Clancy's Oven Cookery

Also by John Clancy

THE JOHN CLANCY BAKING BOOK

Clancy's Oven Cookery

John Clancy & Frances Field

ILLUSTRATIONS BY
Marika

DELACORTE PRESS/ELEANOR FRIEDE

Designed by Ann Spinelli

Library of Congress Cataloging in Publication Data

Clancy, John.
Clancy's Oven cookery.

Includes index.
1. Casserole cookery. 2. Roasting (cookery)
3. Baking. I. Field, Frances, joint author.
II. Title. III. Title: Oven cookery.
TX693.C55   1976   641.7′1   76–17816

ISBN: 0–440–01372–0

For Fred—always encouraging and helpful.
—J.C.

For Eleanor Friede
with whom Michael, our son Jonathan,
our little dog Lisa, and I had so many
glorious times—eating, drinking and making merry.
—F.F.

Contents

Introduction

The story of *Oven Cookery* goes back to New Year's Day, 1967. It was Michael Field, Consulting Editor of TIME-LIFE *Foods of the World* on the phone—at 8:00 A.M. Those who knew the late Michael Field will understand when I say his exuberance and enthusiasm made me forget in seconds the New Year's Eve I'd celebrated the night before. He wanted to explore with me, he said, my joining the TIME-LIFE staff. My good friends the late Paula Peck, an esteemed authority on baking, and James Beard, my teacher and mentor, had recommended me. The assignment sounded challenging, and exactly one month later I found myself in the TIME-LIFE studio beginning an association with the staff that lasted for five years.

As Executive Chef for the *Foods of the World* project, my responsibility was supervision of the adaptation and testing of some 3,000 authentic recipes from all over the world. Consultants from over 25 countries lent their knowledge and expertise to this giant undertaking.

My earlier experience as chef at Chillingsworth on Cape Cod, and later at The Coach House in New York City, my teaching of cooking and baking, none of it could begin to compare with the excitement, stimulation, and inspiration created by this new environment of global food. Food research I'd done in restaurants abroad pales when I recall the variety of dishes from everywhere on earth materializing right there in the studio.

Production of volumes on cuisines from dozens of countries overlapped to meet publication schedules. At such times, the atmosphere of group journalism was pressured, but certainly never dull. It wasn't unusual, for example, to be on the hunt for a Christmas tree in June for a photograph of Christmas cookies due in the fall. Once we needed watermelons in January for a picture of fruits in a book due in June. I remember searching for reindeer steaks in New York City—to cook them smothered in onions as done in the American Northwest—on the very same day I had to find banana leaves in which to steam the chicken, meat, and dough filling for Venezuelan *hallacas centrales*. Without a doubt, TIME-LIFE *Foods of the World*—with Series Editor Richard L. Williams at the helm, Michael in and out of the studio, staff researchers taking notes, photographers' strobe lights flashing, food consultants whipping up classic and exotic dishes—gave me five of the most exciting years in my professional life.

It was a peak experience that broadened the base from which to give cooking demonstrations all over the United States and as far away as Japan. It enriched the repertoire of dishes I teach my students, and surely threads its way throughout this book.

Meeting Frances, Michael Field's wife and coauthor of this book, also took place at that time. Michael introduced us as we waited to board the plane for Montreal and Expo 67. All of us at the studio knew Frances ran "Michael Field's Cooking School" and was an exhibiting artist. On the plane, while Michael discussed recipes with a food researcher for the upcoming volume on Russia, I found myself talking traditional French, Italian, and British dishes with Frances. She and Michael had spent several months on food research the year before, traveling out from Julia Child's house in the South of France where they lived that summer. I remember Frances saying she'd slept in the bed James Beard had vacated at Julia's just a week or two before they arrived. Absorbing vibrations of Jim's knowledge, she said, plus talking food with Michael all day, and with Simca (Simone Beck, coauthor of *Mastering the Art of French Cooking*), who lived next door, probably accounted for her store of information on the subject of food. We laughed quite a lot at that, but when researching food at Expo 67's restaurants, her comments revealed an impeccable taste sensibility refined by experience; Frances is a connoisseur of food. A few years later she and Michael took off for Switzerland, the Benelux countries, Rumania, Bulgaria, and North Africa—a research trip which resulted in their collaboration on the text of TIME-LIFE's *A Quintet of Cuisines*. They teamed up again to write pieces for *Travel & Leisure*. It was clear that Frances observed with an artist's eye, and was a food researcher and writer of first rank.

In the food world, wonders never cease. Commissioned to write "Baking, Sweet and Savory" for *The Great Cooks Cookbook*, whom should I encounter as one of the editors but Frances Field. She had surfaced again in my world, and soon we were reminiscing about Michael and *Foods of the World*. We also got to talking about cooking schools, the difference between Michael's teaching methods and mine, and the questions students asked. She recalled a student asking Michael what the difference was between a stove and an oven. That prompted a flippant remark from me: "Except for baking a pie now and then, or making an occasional roast, most people use ovens for storing pots and pans."

I couldn't forget our conversation, and that night I kept thinking: *ovens*. Thoughts about why I have always found oven-cooking such a great way to work with food brought a flood of memories that went back to childhood days in our summer vacation home on Eastern Long Island. In those days, if my mother had forgotten her rolling pin in New York City, she managed brilliantly with a smooth piece of metal pipe. Pastry was chilled in an old-fashioned icebox, and water came from a hand pump. Pies, roasts, and stews were made in a portable oven set on top of a two-burner kerosene stove. Cooking was a necessity; baking was not. With all the care and attention required to cope with unevenness of heat in that primitive arrangement, this was my initiation into the superior flavor and texture of oven-cooked foods.

In today's ovens food cooks evenly because heat at controlled temperature circulates all around, above, and beneath it. On top of the stove, heat is concentrated under the pot, and the food needs frequent attention. Many dishes made in the oven gain in flavor, and the cooking time is reduced as well.

It struck me suddenly that the oven is a source of heat, beyond the customary four burners, and too few cooks seem to appreciate what an advantage that is. Food that's cooking in the oven is out of the way; the top of the stove is cleared for making sauces to accompany a dish that's baking or roasting. Asking myself why I couldn't remember a book devoted entirely to this way of cooking, I thought the reason lay in the limited number of dishes one could make. But then I realized how many *could* be made—all categories of food in those baking dishes, casseroles, and pie pans. I could see them unreeling in my mind as if I were watching a movie.

I saw at once that foods one would serve with drinks could be made in the oven—fish and shellfish, filled pastries, pâté, to name a few. And what, I asked myself, is more gratifying than a baked soup with fresh homemade bread? "Something as simple as that," I said out loud, "would be a gastronomic event for guests!" Fish, meat, and poultry dishes, vegetable dishes; ideas seemed to come in an endless stream. I had to tell Frances our quips and jokes had produced the wildest fantasy. When I was about halfway through my "movie," she interrupted excitedly. "That is indeed a *book*!" As I had said countless times at the TIME-LIFE studio, there's no such thing as a "new dish" until there are new ingredients. What one can invent are adaptations, variations, and different combinations of ingredients to produce a "new" flavor, or "new" texture in a "new" shape. By adding a traditional touch characteristic of a dish from one cuisine to an appropriate one from another, one invents a "different" dish. "I'll make additions to traditions," I said.

Once I realized we were taking the idea seriously, the immensity of the undertaking suddenly floored me; I began to see insurmountable hurdles. Pondering the need to do some research in food chemistry, Frances recalled that Michael had often spoken to Dr. Paul Buck at Cornell University's Department of Food Science. Then I remembered having called Dr. Buck many times myself from the TIME-LIFE studio, as had a number of the staff researchers. He had always enjoyed giving us information, and he seemed to know everything about food from the time seeds went into the ground to when they appeared as processed products all wrapped up for sale on the supermarket shelves. As our book progressed, we talked to Dr. Buck a lot. He not only helped us clarify information, but gave me a great "new" technique to share. "Here's an idea for when you make two loaves of bread," he said. "Before the last rise, aim for the middle of the dough, and give it a karate chop right down to the work surface. It shears and seals the dough at the same time. And it's fun!" I thought I knew everything there was to know about making and baking bread, and said so to Dr. Buck. "It's a new one on me," I admitted, "but I'll try it. I have to be convinced." Thinking of the reams of literature on making bread and how much "fun" it is, I wasn't too eager to use that worn-out phrase again. But I tried his technique. It worked, and using the karate chop *is* fun! It also keeps the carbon dioxide bubbles in the dough where they belong, instead of letting them escape into the air. I called Dr. Buck to tell him I was convinced. He was delighted. "Call it Clancy's Karate Chop," he offered generously.

Frances helped me over the last hurdle. For the life of me, I couldn't think of a suitable title for this book. "Keep it simple," she advised. "Call it just what it is: *Clancy's Oven Cookery*." And so we did. We hope you enjoy these oven-made dishes as much as we enjoyed assembling the recipes for you.

John Clancy
New York City

Utensils

Don't be alarmed by the number of utensils on this list; you may already own quite a few of them. For success with the recipes in this book, you do need them all. To limit the supply of heavy equipment you will need, the recipes have been so devised that many of them are made in casseroles and baking dishes of the same dimensions.

What can't be stressed too much is the importance of the right kind of pot or pan, and that it be of the right size. Just as important is its weight. When a recipe calls specifically for a "heavy" skillet or casserole, the success of the dish depends on its "heaviness" since such equipment retains heat and evenly distributes it through the ingredients it contains. The purpose of oven cookery is to let the oven work for you, but an oven set at a specific degree of temperature for a specific length of time can't be relied upon if the equipment used is not what the recipe calls for.

This doesn't mean that it isn't possible to make the necessary adjustments to control cooking and baking in equipment of incorrect size and weight, if you know exactly what you're doing. But even under such circumstances, there is no assurance of success. Suppose that, when making Stuffed Cabbage, you were to use a larger baking dish than the shallow one (10 × 14 × 2 inches) called for. In a larger dish, the sauce would reduce more quickly because its larger surface would accumulate a greater amount of heat. It would require watching, because in an unguarded moment the sauce might scorch. The same goes for casseroles which are too big, too small, too shallow, or too deep in relation to those called for; casseroles of the wrong size used indiscriminately can ruin a dish. It's safer to improvise when cooking on top of the stove than when baking in the oven. There's time to try to make adjustments and better control the mishaps that come from using inappropriate equipment. But, then, cooking on top of the stove requires much more of your attention.

Perhaps the first little piece of equipment you should look for among your utensils is a simple ruler. A ruler is a *must* not only for measuring pastry, but before deciding what you may or may not need from this list, you should measure also the cooking and baking equipment you have, as well as the size of your oven. Be sure that any utensils you have to buy will fit.

Whatever you buy should be of the best quality, and cooking and baking equipment of the best quality is the sturdiest and therefore expensive—and not always pretty. But expensive as it may be, it will probably cost less than the fashionably styled decorative utensils to be found in most "cookware" and "gourmet" shops. The heavy-duty equipment every fine cook needs can best be found in restaurant supply houses.

"Restaurant supply house" should not scare you off. I advise my students to turn to the yellow pages in the telephone book, locate the restaurant supply house nearest them, and go shopping there at once. While these suppliers are used to dealing with restaurant owners and usually sell equipment at wholesale prices, often they are willing to deal with individuals at prices somewhat higher. Still, these prices will not be as high as those asked in retail shops, and usually are much lower.

When you shop for utensils, remember that the heavier they are the more even the temperature will be and, therefore, the better your finished dishes will be, too. I'm still using mixing bowls my grandmother owned in the early 1900s. Pots, pans, cookie sheets, and jelly-roll pans my mother bought in the 1920s and '30s are among my most prized and cherished possessions. They were sturdily made of good materials and have endured the test of frequent use through all these years.

UTENSILS LIST

FOR MEASURING

liquid measuring cups: 1, 2, and 4 cup
dry measuring cups: $\frac{1}{4}$, $\frac{1}{3}$, $\frac{1}{2}$, and 1 cup
metal measuring spoons: $\frac{1}{4}$ teaspoon, $\frac{1}{2}$ teaspoon, 1 teaspoon, and
    1 tablespoon

BAKING PANS AND COOKIE SHEETS

two cookie sheets 14 × 16 inches
three 9-inch layer-cake pans
one jelly-roll pan 11 × 16 inches
one 12-cup muffin tin, each cup holding 4 ounces
one 9-inch tart tin with removable bottom (quiche pan)
one large shallow roasting pan about 12 × 18 inches with rack to
    fit one loaf pan 9 × 5 × 3 inches
one 4-cup ring mold

BAKING DISHES

one baking dish 7 × 12 × 2 inches
one baking dish 10 × 14 × 2 inches
one baking dish 6 × 10 × 2 inches
one 2-quart soufflé dish
one 10-inch glass pie dish
one pâté dish, 4 × 10 inches, $2\frac{1}{2}$ inches deep, enameled cast iron,
    with tight-fitting cover

SKILLETS AND SAUTÉ PANS

one 12-inch heavy sauté pan
one 10-inch iron skillet
one 12-inch iron skillet
one 8-inch iron skillet

SAUCEPANS AND POTS

one 1-quart heavy saucepan
one 2-quart heavy saucepan
one 2-cup heavy saucepan
one 4-quart pot

CASSEROLES

4 to 6 quarts, with tight-fitting cover, preferably enameled cast
    iron
8 to 10 quarts, with tight-fitting cover, preferably enameled cast
    iron

MIXING BOWLS

glass or stainless-steel mixing bowls from 2-cup to 2-quart capacity

MISCELLANEOUS

ruler
rubber spatulas, small and large
wooden spoons, 8, 10, and 14 inches
metal icing spatula
one or two metal pancake spatulas
wire whisks, 8-inch and 12-inch
pastry scraper
two pastry brushes, 1 large and 1 small
three wire cake racks
one 5-pound rolling pin, measuring 24 to 26 inches long, including
    the handles

cookie cutters, 1 inch and 3 inches
one 6-inch fine-meshed sieve
one small wire (juice) strainer
one large (6-inch) wire strainer
one 5-cup flour sifter
one 10-inch colander
one 4-sided grater
food mill
10-inch nylon pastry bag
No. 4 star tube
pastry wheel
timer
pepper mill
chopping knife
paring knife
slicer (for meat)
bread knife
oven thermometer
meat thermometer
metal poultry skewers
trussing cord

ELECTRIC EQUIPMENT

electric blender
electric mixer, portable or standard

Menu Suggestions

For successful entertaining with dishes from *Clancy's Oven Cookery*, it's important to build your own menus around one of its main-course dishes.

These menus have been planned so that suggested dishes can be easily executed by those of you who have only one oven. If you have two ovens, you might like to select a second baked dish—Rice Pilaf or Potatoes Anna, for example, in place of rice steamed on top of the stove.

When reading the introductions to the recipes as well as the notes that follow, you will find the dishes that can be made days ahead of time—some even months ahead—to be frozen and quickly reheated. Others, made earlier in the day, may be served later at room temperature.

Tossed green salad is suggested often because this simple dish is suitable with almost all main courses. In fact, a tossed salad may take the place of a green vegetable, or may be served as a separate course along with an appropriate cheese.

If you are pressed for time, the dessert you serve is important. Since it's the last dish on your menu, it will be the first one remembered. If you must buy it, think first; shop carefully for seasonal fruits and melons, and be sure they're ripe. Buy only the best cheeses. Ice cream should be of the finest quality, and cookies bought only at the most reputable bakeries.

If you've spent spare time to bake and freeze a dessert, all that's required is moving it to the refrigerator to serve when needed.

Used to best advantage, your oven and your freezer can produce true kitchen magic.

More and more each year, California wines have been accepted with great acclaim by international connoisseurs. And frequently they are less expensive than their imported counterparts. California labels can be used for all wines recommended in the menu suggestions that follow.

MENU SUGGESTIONS

DINNER PARTIES

1.

Braised Tongue
Boiled New Potatoes
Tossed Green Salad
Baked Pears
Wine: Burgundy

2.

Beef Broth
Roast Ducks with Cranberry Sauce
Steamed Rice
Tossed Green Salad
Sherbet with Assorted Cookies
Wine: Zinfandel

3.

Roast Filet of Beef on Puff Pastry Rounds
Baked Tomato Halves, served at room temperature

Tossed Green Salad
Lemon Dacquoise
Wine: Cabernet

4.
Roast Pork with Mustard Glaze
Potato Cheese Casserole, served at room temperature
Tiny Peas
Upside-Down Apple Pie
Wine: Johannisberg Riesling

5.
Mushroom Barley Soup
Stuffed Cabbage
Boiled New Potatoes in Jackets
Caraway Rye Bread
Cheesecake
Beverage: Beer

LUNCHEONS

1.
Chicken Pie
Tossed Green Salad
Fresh Pineapple with Kirsch
Wine: Fumé Blanc

2.
Crudités
Baked Scallops
Steamed Rice, Tossed with Chopped Fresh Parsley
Blueberry Dumpling Pie
Wine: Pinot Chardonnay

3.
Country Pâté
Chicken in White-Wine Sauce
Buttered Noodles

Tossed Green Salad
Fresh Strawberries with Framboise
Wine: Chablis

4.
Roast Chicken Bijou
Sliced Tomatoes with Oil and Vinegar Dressing
Buttered Steamed Rice
Melon, or Frozen Chocolate-Coffee Torte
Wine: Fumé Blanc

5.
Beef Broth
Filet of Sole in a Tart Shell
Tossed Green Salad
Poached Pears
Wine: Pinot Chardonnay

PICNICS

1.
Country Pâté
Cold Roast Chicken Bijou
Cherry Tomatoes
Scallions
Endive
Cucumbers
French Bread
Assorted Fresh Fruits
Wine: Chablis

2.
Mushroom-Onion Cocktail Turnovers, cool
Stuffed Breast of Veal, chilled
Baked Tomato Halves, cool
French Bread
Fresh Pears and Bel Paese Cheese
Wine: Beaujolais (lightly chilled), or Fumé Blanc

COCKTAIL PARTIES
(Select according to size of party)

1.

Baked Ham in a Pastry Cape
Assorted Mustards
Assorted Breads, thinly sliced
Raw Vegetables with a Flavored Mayonnaise Dip
Selection of Baked Shellfish
Country Pâté

2.

Pizza-filled Ramekins
Raw Vegetables with a Flavored Mayonnaise Dip
Buttered Nuts
Sliced Country Pâté on bread fingers

Pastry

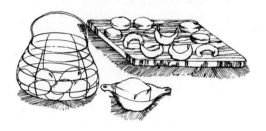

If this is your first attempt at making pastry, or another try after many failures, you're in for a surprise. You don't need inborn talent, a mysterious touch, or revelations of family culinary secrets. Everything in pastry making, even when it appears to be miraculous, is based on simple logic. If you have a passion for eating, cooking, or just poking around the kitchen, you can make pastry.

Try not to blame the instructions if they don't seem to work the first time; they will the next. You may have missed a step, or done one incorrectly. Before you start, tell yourself this truth: a pastry made in your own kitchen is better than any you buy, if only because of the good ingredients you know are in it.

Good ingredients are called for in all the recipes in this book, and some recipes require a specific pastry to enhance a specific dish. All the pastries you'll need for any recipe in the book are in this section. You'll be able to make casings for sauced fillings, meats, fish, fowl; shells for fruits, creams, and other delectables. Your first pastry may be a little less than elegant, but it will be much more than merely edible.

INGREDIENTS, AND HOW TO MEASURE
THEM ACCURATELY

All the recipes in this book have been based on carefully balanced amounts of ingredients. If you measure carelessly the balances are thrown off. Take the trouble to measure correctly and accurately. It will produce delicious-tasting results.

Butter Use only unsalted butter in all recipes. Salt tends to draw out moisture and affects the action of ingredients on each other. Inspect the wrapper; be certain it doesn't read "Sweet Butter," and in small print "Lightly Salted." The salt called for in all recipes has been carefully planned to give just the right amount of seasoning. Salt in the butter will make an oversalted dish.

Some wrappers have markings to indicate the equivalent in tablespoons, but most of them are folded over so that the markings can confuse rather than help you. The following way of measuring is more accurate. Use it as a guide.

$\frac{1}{4}$-pound stick of butter = 8 tablespoons
$\frac{1}{4}$-pound stick, cut into halves = 2 pieces, each
equivalent to 4 tablespoons

When an ingredient list calls for "chilled" butter, be sure it has been chilled first in the refrigerator before you cut it to measure.

Flour Use only all-purpose flour, unless otherwise indicated in the recipe. Never sift it, unless called for in the recipe.

Measure flour this way for accuracy and economy: Lay out a piece of wax paper on your work surface, and set on it the dry measuring cup you need. Spoon the flour into the cup but overfill it. Never press flour into the cup; never tamp it down. With the back of a knife blade, lightly level off excess flour from edge to edge of the cup. To save excess flour, lift the wax paper, hold it like a funnel, and pour back into the container.

Vegetable shortening Always use solid emulsified vegetable shortening (*not* margarine); it consists of beads of fat interlaced with air and traces of water. When combined with more water, it spreads the fat uniformly through the flour. This makes pastry of more predictable texture.

Measure the shortening this way for accuracy and economy: Dip a standard metal measuring spoon into the can of shortening and overfill the spoon. With the back of a knife blade, level it off to the edges of the spoon and return the excess to the can. With your index finger, push the shortening out of the bowl of the spoon into the receptacle you are using.

When an ingredient list calls for "chilled" vegetable shortening, measure it first into a dish, and make sure you place it in the refrigerator when the instructions call for this step.

Refrigerating pastry for 1 hour before rolling it out keeps the butter and shortening chilled. But just as important, it allows the gluten in the flour to "relax." This makes for a manageable dough that is easy to roll out, and prevents its cracking and breaking. All pastry is easier to roll if chilled first.

CREAM CHEESE PASTRY

If you are a novice baker, the best way to begin is to get your hands into the raw ingredients. This recipe has everything to recommend it, since nothing can go wrong. Unlike pastry calling for ice water, which needs some attention, this one requires no water at all. By thoroughly mixing together textures as different from each other as butter, flour, and cream cheese, your hands will instantly learn how separate ingredients change into a smooth dough.

Sweet or savory, this is a delicately flavored, light pastry.

> 1½ cups all-purpose flour
> ½ teaspoon salt (plus 2 teaspoons sugar *for sweet pastry*)
> 6 tablespoons unsalted butter, chilled
> 6 tablespoons (3-ounce package) cream cheese

Place the flour in a medium-sized bowl. Scatter the salt over the flour. (For sweet pastry, scatter the sugar over, too.) Add the butter and cheese; with your hands combine the ingredients by kneading them together until thoroughly blended. Shape the pastry into a ball and use the pastry ball to pick up any bits clinging to the bowl or to your hands.

Lay out a piece of plastic wrap, dust it lightly with flour, and place the ball of pastry on it. With the flat of your hand, press the ball into a thick cake. Shape the sides of the cake into a round and dust all exposed sides lightly with flour (to keep the pastry from sticking). Wrap it, and chill in the refrigerator for 1 hour before using.

NOTES:
REFRIGERATOR STORAGE: Keeps safely for 3 days.
FREEZER STORAGE: Keeps safely for 3 to 4 months, if wrapped carefully so as to be airtight. To use, remove from freezer the night before, and place in refrigerator.

FLAKY PASTRY

If you do a few little things beforehand, you can make this pastry easily and without interruption.

There are sound reasons for everything you do when making Flaky Pastry:

Dry your hands before combining the ingredients because damp fingers dissolve flour, make it sticky, and prevent its incorporating the butter and shortening.

Chill the butter and shortening so they will not soften too much when being combined with the flour. For the same reason, work quickly, but not so quickly that you don't watch what you're doing. Rub the ingredients together only between your thumbs and the ends of your fingers; they are usually the coolest parts of your hands. Oversoftening of butter and shortening makes the mixture into oily paste rather than airy granules. Oily paste bakes to firm, chewy pastry; granules bake to one that is light, delicate, and flaky.

Because too much water toughens pastry and causes it to shrink while baking, it is worth your while to measure water accurately. The 4 tablespoons called for are usually just enough, but the exact amount depends on the moisture in the flour, which can vary from bag to bag. By measuring off 2 extra tablespoons of water into a dish and adding it by droplets you control the amount you need.

> 4 tablespoons unsalted butter, chilled
> 4 tablespoons emulsified vegetable shortening, chilled
> 4 to 6 tablespoons ice water
> 1½ cups all-purpose flour
> ¼ teaspoon salt

Cut half of a ¼-pound stick of chilled butter into slices and place them in a dish. Into the same dish, measure off the vegetable shortening. Place in the refrigerator until ready to use.

Prepare the ice water: run cold water into a liquid measuring cup. Add some ice cubes, and set the cup nearby. (When you need it, the water will be cold enough to use.)

Place the flour in a medium-sized bowl. Scatter the salt over the flour; add the butter and shortening. First dry your hands, then, working quickly, rub the ingredients together only between your thumbs and the ends of your fingers. The mixture will turn into coarse separate pieces, then into granules.

As the granules become smaller, look for any large pieces; from time to time, with palms up and fingers apart, run your hands lightly and quickly through the granules. Lift, then let them flow back between your fingers into the bowl. When you spot large pieces, rub each one, as described, until all granules are fairly uniform in size.

One tablespoon at a time, sprinkle 4 tablespoons of the ice water over all the granules. Combine the water and granules, using only your thumbs and the ends of your fingers; this takes only a few seconds. Now, with cupped hands, gather all the dough into a ball. If the dough crumbles, measure the additional 2 tablespoons of ice water into a dish, dip in your fingertips, and add water by droplets to the dry-looking areas, using only as much as you need to help you shape the ball. Use the ball of pastry to pick up any bits of dough clinging to the bowl or to your hands.

Lay out a piece of plastic wrap, dust it lightly with flour, and place the ball on it. With the flat of your hand, press it into a thick cake. Shape the sides to form a round and dust all exposed sides lightly with flour. Wrap it, and chill in the refrigerator for 1 hour before using.

NOTES:
For a larger amount, as in Cocktail Turnovers (p. 64), increase the ingredients
   to 1½ recipes as follows:

> 2¼ cups all-purpose flour
> ¼ teaspoon salt
> 6 tablespoons unsalted butter, chilled
> 6 tablespoons emulsified vegetable shortening, chilled
> 6 to 8 tablespoons ice water

Follow directions exactly as written for the basic recipe.

REFRIGERATOR STORAGE: Keeps safely for 3 days.
FREEZER STORAGE: Keeps safely for 3 to 4 months, if wrapped carefully so as to
   be airtight. To use, remove from freezer the night before, and place in refrigerator.

A PREBAKED TART SHELL

Before filling a tart shell, the shell must be prebaked for 12 to 14 minutes; this prevents absorption of the filling during the final baking of the tart. The following instructions describe how to line a tart tin (often called a quiche pan) with flaky pastry, and how to prebake a tart shell.

Make Flaky Pastry (p. 25), wrap, and chill. Remove pastry from refrigerator, unwrap, and place on a lightly floured surface. Lightly flour the top of the pastry and your rolling pin. Roll out the pastry into a circular shape, always rolling out from the center and ending each stroke just short of the edge so as not to thin out the edge too soon; you need a little thickness to hold when you turn it. Never roll back toward the center. Turn the pastry clockwise from time to time to test if it is sticking to the surface; if it sticks, flour lightly underneath. Continue rolling out the pastry until it is 1/8 inch thick.

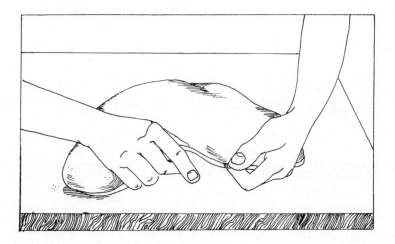

Lining a tart tin with pastry

Set a 9-inch tart tin with removable bottom alongside the rolled-out pastry. Place the rolling pin on the part of the pastry which is farthest from you. With the aid of a metal spatula, lift the far edge of the pastry onto the back of the rolling pin. Using your fingertips, lightly press the pastry against the back of the rolling pin, just enough to make it adhere, and roll the pastry toward yourself, making *1 complete turn.*

Lift the pastry-covered rolling pin by the handles, allowing the remainder of the pastry to hang down freely. Suspending the free pastry just above the tin, bring it forward to the edge of the tin nearest you. Let about 1½ inches of this pastry drop over the front edge of the tin and lie on the work surface. Now, unrolling away

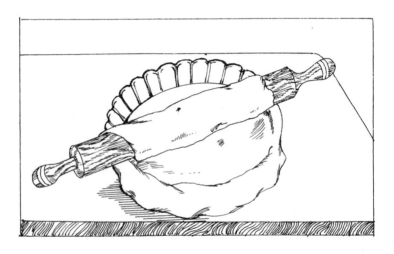

from yourself, let the pastry fall slackly into the tin. Keep the pin *above* the edge when unrolling; the weight of the pin *on* the edge can cut the pastry. There should be an overhang of about 1½ inches of pastry all around the tin.

To make the pastry conform to the sides of the tin, work with a light touch, never stretching the pastry. Draw from the overhang for any extra amount you may need. To start, lift an edge of the overhang with the fingertips of one hand, hold it loosely, and, with the index finger of your other hand, press the pastry gently against the inside of the tin. Turn the tin from time to time, feeding in the overhang as you need it to line the sides. To sever the excess pastry neatly, set the rolling pin on the edge of the tin and roll over it; the excess will fall away. Cover the lined tin with plastic wrap and chill in the refrigerator for 1 hour before prebaking.

To prebake the tart shell

Preheat oven to 400° F.

Measure off a length of wax paper over the tin of pastry. Set the paper on the pastry and pour into it 2 cups of uncooked rice; this keeps the pastry from puffing up. Place the weighted tin on the lower middle shelf of the oven and bake for 12 to 14 minutes (set your timer), or until the edge of the pastry is pale brown.

Remove the tin to a wire rack. Lift the rice-filled paper from the tart shell. (Store the rice; it can be used again when you prebake other tart shells.) Let the tart shell cool to room temperature before filling.

NOTES:

FREEZER STORAGE: *Do NOT freeze a prebaked tart shell*; when filled and baked it will be soggy. Freeze only unbaked pastry-lined tart tins. These keep safely for 3 to 4 months if wrapped carefully so as to be airtight.

To prebake a frozen unbaked tart shell, first preheat oven to 400° F. Unwrap the lined tin, and proceed exactly as described for an unbaked tart shell that is not frozen.

Some recipes may call for a fully baked tart shell. In this case, remove the rice-filled paper after the shell has baked for 12 minutes, prick the pastry with the tines of a fork and let the shell bake for an additional 8 to 10 minutes or until the entire pastry is a pale brown.

PUFF PASTRY

Puff pastry is one of the greatest inventions in pastry making. It consists of layers of butter and dough, which rise as they bake and turn into countless buttery flakes.

If you would like to know a little about what accounts for this fascinating phenomenon, read the Notes at the end of the recipe. But no matter how informed you are, all chemistry will be forgotten when you taste the delicacy you've made, because puff pastry is definitely a taste thrill.

> $4\frac{1}{2}$ cups all-purpose flour
> $1\frac{1}{4}$ pounds unsalted butter (5 sticks), chilled
> 1 cup ice water
> $\frac{1}{2}$ teaspoon salt
> Additional flour as needed

You will need 2 large mixing bowls in which to combine the flour and butter in different amounts and in different ways. In one of the bowls, place $\frac{1}{2}$ cup of the flour. Remove 4 of the $\frac{1}{4}$-pound sticks of butter from the refrigerator and cut them, one stick at a time, into approximately $\frac{1}{2}$-inch cubes, dropping the cubes by the handful onto the flour as they are cut. With your hands, toss the cubes lightly in the flour until each cube is evenly coated on all sides. Without removing the excess flour, place the bowl of cubes in the refrigerator to chill for at least 15 minutes (set your timer). Prepare ice water by running cold water into a 2-cup glass liquid measuring cup, with ice cubes added. Have an empty 1-cup liquid measuring cup handy.

Place the 4 cups of flour in the second bowl. Remove the remaining $\frac{1}{4}$-pound stick of butter from the refrigerator and cube it *into* the flour. Immediately, fill the 1-cup measure with ice water and pour it over the flour and butter. Scatter the salt over the ingredients, and with both hands energetically work them together, kneading and squeezing to combine them thoroughly. When the mixture begins to stick to your hands and to the bowl, add a little flour and work it in. Continue to knead, adding a little flour at a time until the dough stops sticking and becomes a mass.

Lightly flour your work surface and the dough. Put the dough on the work surface, and continue to knead it. If it sticks, again add flour, a little at a time, to both dough and work surface, and knead the dough until it no longer sticks. Shape the dough into a ball, and dust it lightly with flour. Wrap it in wax paper, and place it in the refrigerator.

Remove the bowl of floured butter cubes from the refrigerator. Quickly, with both hands, combine the cubes with the flour and knead until the ingredients are thoroughly blended and smooth.

Shape this flour-butter mixture into a rough square. Using a ruler as a guide, shape the mixture with your hands or a pastry

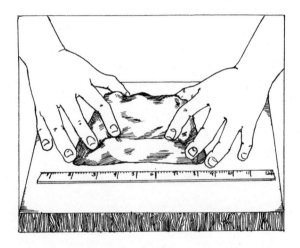

scraper into a neat 4-inch square measuring approximately $1\frac{1}{2}$ inches thick. Lay out a piece of wax paper, and dust it lightly with flour. Place the square on it, and dust all exposed sides lightly with flour. Wrap it, and chill in the refrigerator for 30 minutes.

Remove the ball of dough from the refrigerator and unwrap it. Dust the work surface lightly with flour, and place the ball on it. With a knife make a crisscross cut $\frac{1}{2}$ inch deep into the top of the ball. Press the heel of your hand into the cut and, one at a time,

push out each corner of the dough; it will go quite naturally into the shape of a four-leaf clover.

Dust your rolling pin lightly with flour, and roll out only the leaves. Do *not* roll over the padlike center at all. Roll back and forth on the length of each leaf (if it sticks, flour lightly under-

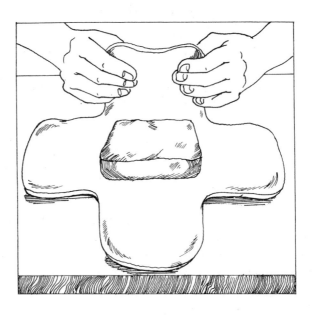

neath), extending each one until the dough now resembles diagonal strips crossed like an X, each diagonal measuring 17 inches from end to end (including the padlike center).

Remove the 4-inch butter square from the refrigerator, unwrap, and place it on the padlike center of the crossed strips. One at a time, bring each strip over the square, pressing down so that each

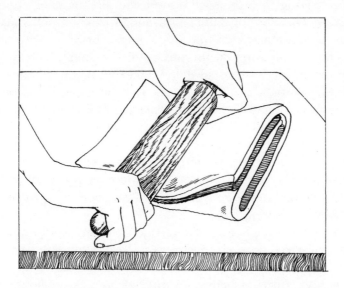

one overlaps and adheres to the one beneath. When the square is completely enclosed in the dough, turn this "package" over, and with the flat of your hand, press it into a 7-inch square. Lay out a piece of wax paper and dust it lightly with flour. Place the 7-inch square on it and dust the exposed sides lightly with flour. Wrap it, and place in the refrigerator to "rest" and chill for 30 minutes (set your timer).

Remove the chilled 7-inch square from the refrigerator. Dust the work surface lightly with flour. Unwrap the square. Dust it lightly with flour, and begin to roll it out into a rectangle. Evenly distributing your weight on the handles of the rolling pin, roll it on the dough all the way to the edges, first away from yourself and then back toward yourself, lifting the dough with your hands or a pastry scraper from time to time to see if it's sticking. If it sticks, dust underneath lightly with flour. Watch for butter breaking through the dough as you roll; if it does, immediately add flour *heavily* to the spot, and roll it in with your pin. Continue to roll out the dough until the rectangle measures 12 inches wide and 21 inches long.

Fold the rectangle into thirds, like a letter, to create 3 layers of dough: starting with the edge nearest you, lift the dough and fold it over, leaving the top 7 inches of dough exposed. This makes 2 layers. As you make each fold, use a pastry brush to dust off any excess flour remaining on the surface of the dough. Lift the edge of the remaining 7 inches of dough and fold it toward yourself so that it lies on top of the first 2 layers. Lay out a piece of *aluminum foil* and dust it lightly with flour. Place the folded dough on it and dust the exposed sides lightly with flour.   **1st turn**

Mark a piece of scrap paper with 5 diagonals. *Cross off one* as an indicator that you have just finished rolling and folding the dough *once*. Wrap the dough, tucking the piece of paper in the foil. Place the dough in the refrigerator to "rest" and chill for 30 minutes (set your timer).

Remove the dough from the refrigerator, unwrap it, and place it with a narrow open end facing you. Roll it out just as you did before, but this time to a rectangle measuring 14 × 24 inches. Fold it into thirds as before, dusting off any excess flour on the surface of the dough.   **2nd turn**

Cross off another diagonal on the scrap paper, and tuck it into the aluminum foil as you wrap the dough. Place the dough in the refrigerator to "rest" and chill for 30 minutes (set your timer).

Roll out and fold the dough, exactly as you have just done, *3 times more*, letting it "rest" and chill for 30 minutes between each rolling.

After the last folding (the 5th), chill the wrapped dough in the refrigerator for 2 hours before using.

NOTES:
See Pastry Scraps and Fleurons (p. 36), if there is any leftover dough after preparing your selected recipe.
REFRIGERATOR STORAGE: Keeps safely for 3 days.

FREEZER STORAGE: Keeps safely for 3 to 4 mouths, if wrapped carefully so as to be airtight. To use, remove from freezer the night before, and place in refrigerator.

To use only a portion, remove dough from freezer to refrigerator. Defrost until dough can be sliced. Rewrap unused portion, making it airtight, and return it to freezer.

If you're curious, take a close look at a slice of your puff pastry, baked or unbaked. You will see countless tissue-thin layers topping each other. Magnified, it may remind you of rock stratification, but be assured, your pastry will be tender, delicate, and flaky. This achievement is the result of many steps correctly done, but an essential one is allowing the dough to "rest" and chill for 30 minutes between rollings. Gluten, a sticky protein substance in flour, is agitated by the kneading and rolling. It can "overdevelop" if not allowed to rest and chill during these 30-minute periods. The result would be an unmanageable, rubbery, and resistant dough. Why take the chance? Letting the gluten "relax" ensures smooth, easy rolling.

The rollings and foldings multiply the layers endlessly. The water you add— in addition to moisture in the large amounts of flour and butter—turns to steam when subjected to the heat of the oven. The steam pushes up the layers, then evaporates, leaving fine air spaces, and the flour absorbs the butter. But if you ignore butter breaking through the dough when you roll it, if you don't flour and roll it back in, both steam and butter can no longer do what they should. Steam would "escape," instead of pushing up the layers, and butter would melt into the oven instead of being absorbed by the flour.

PUFF PASTRY SCRAPS

Puff pastry scraps can be rolled out and used for making Puff Pastry Rounds (p. 37) or for *Fleurons*. First, the scraps should be correctly stacked.

No matter what size or shape, stack the scraps one on top of the other, but no more than 1 inch high. If you plan to use the stack of scraps the same day, dust a piece of aluminum foil lightly with flour, set the pastry on it, and dust its surface lightly with flour. Wrap, and chill for at least 1 hour before rolling out.

FLEURONS

These small puff pastry tidbits are used as garnitures for sauced dishes such as Chicken Braised in Red Wine (p. 136), Chicken in White-Wine Sauce (p. 134), and Braised Tongue (p. 158).

To make *fleurons*, remove the stacked scraps from the refrigerator, unwrap, and place on a lightly floured surface. Dust the pastry and your rolling pin lightly with flour. Roll out the pastry into a rectangle or square $\frac{1}{4}$ inch thick. Using 2-inch cookie cutters in the shape of crescents, diamonds, or small rounds, cut out the *fleurons*.

Run cold water over a cookie sheet, shake off the excess, and set the *fleurons* on it about 1 inch apart. Place the cookie sheet in the refrigerator for 20 minutes (set your timer), and *preheat oven to 400° F.*

Before baking the *fleurons*, combine 1 egg and 2 tablespoons cream or milk and beat them until well blended. With a pastry brush, paint a film of the mixture just on the top of each *fleuron*; take care that none of it runs down the sides because the egg and milk mixture would seal the pastry and prevent its rising properly.

Place the cookie sheet on the middle shelf of the oven and bake for 10 to 12 minutes (set your timer), or until golden brown. Remove from the oven and slide the *fleurons* onto a wire rack to cool to room temperature.

NOTES:

Fleurons may be stored at room temperature in airtight containers for 3 to 4 days. To warm them, set on a cookie sheet in a hot oven for a few minutes.

Fleurons may be frozen safely for 3 to 4 months if wrapped so as to be airtight. To reheat, remove from the freezer, unwrap, and place them on a cookie sheet. Set them on the middle shelf of a preheated 400° F. oven for 6 to 8 minutes.

PUFF PASTRY ROUNDS

To accompany a heavily sauced dish, Puff Pastry Rounds may be served in place of starchy vegetables such as potatoes or rice. One 3-inch round is considered sufficient for each serving.

Although the recipe calls for a one-quarter portion of the puff pastry recipe, the rounds can be made successfully with the equivalent amount of Puff Pastry Scraps (p. 36).

> ¼ recipe Puff Pastry
> 1 egg
> 2 tablespoons cream or milk

Remove puff pastry from refrigerator, unwrap, and place it on a lightly floured surface. Measure and cut off one quarter of it. Wrap and refreeze the remaining pastry. Lightly flour the surface of the pastry and your rolling pin, and begin to roll the pastry into a rectangle. Evenly distributing your weight on the handles of the rolling pin, roll it on the pastry all the way to the edges— first away from yourself, then back toward yourself. To test for sticking, run a metal spatula underneath the pastry. If it sticks, dust lightly underneath with flour. Continue rolling until the rectangle measures 8 × 10 inches.

With a 3-inch-round cookie cutter, cut out 6 rounds. Run cold water over a large cookie sheet, shake off the excess, and set the rounds on it 1 inch apart. Place the cookie sheet in the refrigerator for 20 minutes (set your timer), and *preheat oven to 400° F.*

Just before baking the rounds, beat the egg and cream (or milk) together until well combined. Using a pastry brush, paint a film of the mixture just on top of each round; take care that none of it runs down the sides because that would prevent the pastry from rising properly.

Set the cookie sheet on the middle shelf of the oven and bake for 10 minutes (set your timer). *Reduce oven heat to 375° F.,* and bake for 4 to 6 minutes, or until the rounds are puffed and brown.

Remove the cookie sheet from the oven. Puff pastry rounds may be served hot from the oven, at room temperature, or warmed. To have them at room temperature, slide them off the cookie sheet onto a wire rack—top side up—to cool. To warm the rounds, see Notes.

NOTES:

Puff pastry rounds may be stored at room temperature in an airtight container for 3 to 4 days. To warm them, set on a cookie sheet in a hot oven for a few minutes.

FREEZER STORAGE: Baked, then wrapped so as to be airtight, rounds can be safely frozen for 3 to 4 months. To reheat, remove from the freezer, unwrap, and place them on a cookie sheet. Set them on the middle shelf of a preheated 400° F. oven for 10 minutes.

PSEUDO PUFF PASTRY

Pseudo Puff Pastry may be used interchangeably with Puff Pastry in the recipes in this book. Rolled out and folded fewer times, Pseudo Puff Pastry has fewer layers, however, so it doesn't rise as high and it isn't as flaky as Puff Pastry.

> 5 cups all-purpose flour
> 1 teaspoon salt
> 1¾ cups ice water
> 1 pound (4 sticks) unsalted butter, chilled
> Additional flour as needed

Place the flour and salt in a large mixing bowl; using a wooden spoon, combine them well. Pour in the ice water all at once; still using the wooden spoon, stir all the ingredients together (scrape in and include any bits adhering to the sides of the bowl) until the flour has absorbed all the liquid. Using your hands, gather the dough and shape it into a ball.

Lightly flour your work surface. Place the ball of dough on it and knead it energetically. If it is sticky, add a little flour and work it in. Continue to knead it, adding flour a little at a time and only when you need it, until the dough no longer sticks and becomes a mass. Shape the dough into a ball and dust it lightly with flour. Wrap it in wax paper, and refrigerate for 15 minutes (set your timer).

To flatten ¼-pound sticks of butter into rectangles 4 × 6 inches

Tear off 4 generous lengths of wax paper. Remove the 4 sticks of chilled butter from the refrigerator and unwrap them. One at a time, center a butter stick horizontally on a sheet of the wax paper. Fold over it an ample piece of the paper from the edge nearest you. With your rolling pin, first press down hard on the paper to flatten the butter beneath, then roll on the paper to shape the butter into a rectangle measuring approximately 4 × 6 inches. If the butter is too hard to flatten, first pound it with the

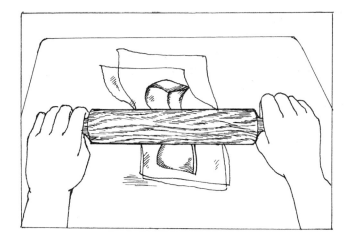

rolling pin to make it more malleable, fold the paper over, and proceed as just described.

After flattening, lift the paper and straighten the sides of the butter so that the rectangle measures exactly 4 × 6 inches. Completely enclose the rectangle in the paper, and place it in the refrigerator. When all the butter sticks have been shaped, wrapped, and placed in the refrigerator, chill them for 15 minutes (set your timer).

Remove the ball of dough from the refrigerator. Dust the work surface lightly with flour. Unwrap the dough, dust it lightly with flour, and begin to roll it out into a rectangle. Evenly distributing your weight on the handles of the rolling pin, roll it on the dough all the way to the edges, first away from yourself, then back toward yourself. Continue rolling it out until the rectangle measures approximately 8 inches wide and 14 to 15 inches long.

Now make a packet consisting of 3 layers of dough-enclosed butter as follows, using a pastry brush to dust off any flour remaining on the dough after making each fold.

Remove 3 of the butter rectangles from the refrigerator and unwrap them. About 4½ inches from the edge of the dough nearest you, place one rectangle of butter horizontally, with its 6-inch side parallel to the 8-inch edge of the dough. Approximately 1 inch of dough will be exposed to the right and left of the butter.

Starting with the edge of dough nearest you, lift and fold it over the butter. Press the extra ½ inch of dough to the dough beneath, closing the butter in. Then press the side edges together fully to enclose the butter. This makes 1 layer of dough-enclosed butter.

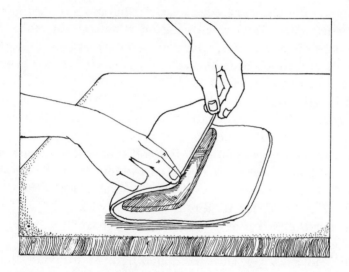

Now place the second rectangle of butter on this layer. Fold *both the layer and the butter over.* Press the edge of the dough to the dough beneath to close this butter in, then press the sides together to enclose it fully. This makes 2 layers.

Place the third rectangle of butter on this layer. Now, bring the exposed dough toward yourself, and fold it over the butter. This makes 3 layers. Once more, press the dough to the dough beneath to close the butter in, then press the side edges together to enclose it fully. Turn the dough over, seam side down, and shape it into a neat rectangular packet.

Again, lightly flour the work surface. Place the packet of dough on it so that a narrow end faces you. Dust the dough lightly with flour, and roll it out just as you did before, *but this time* to a rectangle measuring about 8 inches wide and 12 inches long. Watch for butter breaking through as you roll. If it does, flour the spot heavily, and roll it in.

Remove the fourth rectangle of butter from the refrigerator. Unwrap, then center it on the dough horizontally, its 6-inch sides parallel to the 8-inch edges of dough. There will be about 4 inches of exposed dough at the edge nearest you, and 4 inches more at the farther end. Starting with the edge nearest you, fold the 4 inches of dough over the butter. As before, press the edge of the dough to the dough beneath to close the butter in, then press the side edges together to enclose it fully. Now, lift the edge of the exposed dough and bring it toward yourself so that it lies on top of the enclosed butter beneath. Once more, press the edge of the dough to the dough beneath, then press the side edges together.

Lay out a piece of aluminum foil and dust it lightly with flour. Place the dough, seam side down, on the foil. Dust the surface of the dough lightly with flour. Wrap it, and place it in the refrigerator to "rest" for 15 minutes (set your timer).

Remove the packet of dough from the refrigerator. Flour your work surface lightly. Unwrap the dough, and place it so that a narrow end faces you. Dust the dough lightly with flour, and roll it out just as you did before, *but this time* to a rectangle measuring 14 × 24 inches.

Roll out and fold the dough, exactly as you have just done, *2 more times*, letting it rest 15 minutes between these two steps.

NOTES:

REFRIGERATOR STORAGE: Keeps safely for 3 days.

FREEZER STORAGE: Keeps safely for 3 to 4 months, if wrapped so as to be airtight. To use, remove from freezer the night before, and place in refrigerator.

To use only a portion, remove dough from freezer to refrigerator. Defrost until dough can be sliced. Rewrap unused portion so as to be airtight, and return it to freezer.

To store Pseudo Puff Pastry scraps, no matter what size or shape, stack the scraps one on top of the other, but no more than 1 inch high. If you plan to use the stack of scraps the same day, dust a piece of aluminum foil lightly with flour, set the pastry on it, and dust its surface lightly with flour. Wrap, and chill for at least 1 hour before rolling out.

Treated in like manner, and wrapped airtight, scraps can also be frozen from 3 to 4 months. Before using, place in refrigerator overnight.

Food with Drinks and First Courses

ASSORTED SAVORY PASTRY STICKS

(MAKES 120 STICKS)

PASTRY
2 teaspoons softened butter
1 recipe Pseudo Puff Pastry (p. 39)

GLAZE
1 egg
2 tablespoons milk or water

SEASONINGS
1 tablespoon coarse salt
2 teaspoons caraway seeds mixed with 1 teaspoon coarse
salt
2 teaspoons poppy seeds mixed with 1 teaspoon coarse salt

Lightly grease a cookie sheet 14 × 16 inches with the softened butter, and set it aside.

Remove the chilled pastry from the refrigerator. Dust the work surface lightly with flour. Unwrap the dough, dust it lightly with flour, and roll it out into a rectangle. Evenly distributing your weight on the handles of the rolling pin, roll it on the pastry all the way to the edges—first away from yourself, then back toward yourself. To test for sticking, run a metal spatula underneath the pastry; if it sticks, lightly flour underneath. Continue rolling it out until the rectangle measures 15 × 16 inches. Now and then, line up and straighten the sides of the rectangle with a pastry scraper.

Combine the egg and milk (or water) well by beating them together in a small bowl. With a pastry brush, paint a film of the mixture over the entire surface of the pastry.

With a sharp knife and a ruler as a guide, cut the pastry into thirds horizontally. You will now have 3 pieces equal in size, but *do not separate them.*

Sprinkle the coarse salt generously over the first of the three pieces of the pastry. Sprinkle the caraway and salt mixture over the second, and the poppy-seed and salt mixture over the third.

Place a piece of wax paper over the entire surface of the seasoned pastry. Gently roll over the paper with your rolling pin to press the seasonings into the pastry. Remove and discard the paper.

Using a sharp knife with a ruler as a guide, cut the pastry vertically into 4-inch-wide strips; and, again, horizontally, all the way across, into ½-inch strips. When separated from this gridiron pattern, each pastry strip will measure ½ × 4 inches.

Lift the strips one by one. Using both hands, pick up a strip between thumb and index finger of each hand. Hold it up and give the strip a gentle half-twist to form a spiral stick. If you can manage another half-twist without breaking the strip, do so. Lightly—just enough to make them adhere—press the ends of the strip down onto the cookie sheet. Repeat with the remaining strips, arranging them on the cookie sheet in rows.

Place the cookie sheet in the refrigerator and chill for 20 minutes (set your timer). *Preheat oven to 375° F.*

Place the cookie sheet on the middle shelf of the oven and bake for 10 to 12 minutes, until the pastry sticks are lightly browned.

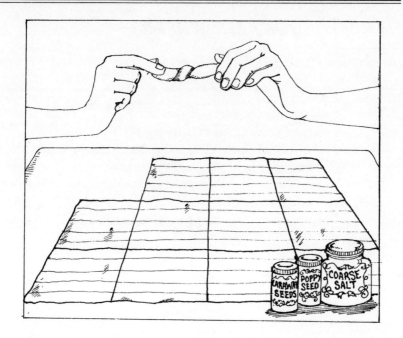

Remove cookie sheet from the oven. With a metal spatula, transfer the sticks to a wire rack. Cool to room temperature before serving.

NOTE:

STORAGE: Store in airtight containers at room temperature; these will keep safely for 2 to 3 days.

HERBED COCKTAIL WAFERS

(MAKES ABOUT 3 DOZEN)

PASTRY
2 teaspoons softened butter
1 recipe Cream Cheese Pastry (p. 24)
2 tablespoons finely chopped fresh chives or freeze-dried
  chives
2 tablespoons finely chopped fresh chervil, or 1 teaspoon
  dried chervil
1 tablespoon finely chopped fresh tarragon, or 1 teaspoon
  dried tarragon

GLAZE
1 egg
2 tablespoons cream or milk
Coarse salt

Lightly grease a cookie sheet 14 × 16 inches with the softened butter and set aside.

Remove the chilled pastry from the refrigerator, unwrap, and place it in a bowl. Add the chives, chervil, and tarragon. With your hands, combine the ingredients until they are thoroughly blended and can be shaped into a ball.

Place the ball of pastry on a lightly floured surface. With the flat of your hand press it into a thick cake. Shape it into a round, and dust it lightly with flour. Lightly flour your rolling pin. Always begin to roll on the pastry from the center outward, ending each stroke just short of the edge. From time to time, lift the edge and turn the pastry clockwise to test if it is sticking; if it sticks, lightly flour underneath. If the rolling pin sticks, lightly flour both rolling pin and the surface of the pastry. Continue rolling out the pastry, turning it clockwise, until it is ⅛ inch thick, including the edge.

With a 2- to 2½-inch cookie cutter, press out circles of pastry as close together as you can. Distribute the cut-out wafers evenly on the cookie sheet. Gather up the scraps, quickly shape them into a ball, then press the ball into a cake with the flat of your hand. Shape it into a round and roll it out again as just described. Press out more circles, and add them to the cookie sheet. Repeat the whole procedure until all the pastry is used.

Preheat oven to 375° F.

Place the cookie sheet in refrigerator and chill the wafers for 20 minutes (set your timer).

Just before baking the wafers, beat the egg and cream (or milk) together well. With a pastry brush, paint a film of the mixture on top of each wafer, then sprinkle each one generously with coarse salt.

Place on the middle shelf of the oven and bake for 10 minutes. Remove from the oven. Transfer the wafers from the cookie sheet to a wire rack with a metal spatula. Let them cool to room temperature before serving.

NOTES:

If your kitchen is too warm, the pastry may oversoften and make it difficult to reroll the pastry and press out all the rounds. Should this happen at any time during the procedure, gather the pastry into a ball, wrap it in wax paper, and chill in the refrigerator for 10 to 15 minutes. Before rolling it out, place it on a lightly floured surface, press it with the flat of your hand into a cake, then shape it into a round, and roll it out as you did before.

STORAGE: Store in airtight containers at room temperature; these will keep safely for up to 1 week.

TOAST RAMEKINS WITH SAUCED FILLINGS

Simply and quickly made, Toast Ramekins are glossy and golden brown, crisp, leakproof, small edible containers for sauced fillings. Easily made in spare moments, they freeze safely for months. Transferred from freezer to a hot oven, they finish in 5 minutes.

(MAKES 12 RAMEKINS)

> 12 slices of fresh white bread, homemade or store-bought, sliced no more than 1/4 inch thick
> 2 to 3 tablespoons melted butter

To make the bread more flexible and less porous, roll a rolling pin backward and forward *once* over each slice of bread. Use a 3-inch cookie cutter to cut one round from each slice of bread. (Remaining bread and crusts may be used to make bread crumbs.)

Construct the ramekins one at a time in the 12 cups of a muffin tin with 4-ounce cups. With a pastry brush, apply melted butter over the entire surface of one side of a bread round. Buttered side down, place the round over a muffin cup; with your fingertips gently press the round into the bottom of the cup to form a bread shell, 1/2 inch deep, to hold about 1 tablespoon of filling. Pressing lightly with the tip of a forefinger, mold the bottom and sides to conform to the shape of the cup. Mold and flatten the top edge into a neat rim. (You don't want a lopsided shell.)

Preheat oven to 425° F.

Repeat the procedure with the remaining rounds. Place the muffin tin on the middle shelf of the oven and prebake for 12 minutes, or until the rims are lightly browned.

When cool enough to handle, transfer the ramekins to paper towels and let stand until they are drained of any excess butter.

Double the recipe to make 24 ramekins.

Here are some fillings for Toast Ramekins. These crisp containers are sure to inspire you to invent some fillings of your own. Be sure to use sauces as thick in texture as those which follow. A thin sauce will permeate the ramekin, oversoften it, and cause it to disintegrate.

CURRIED SHRIMP FILLING

(MAKES FILLING FOR 12 RAMEKINS)

SHRIMPS
6 medium-sized shrimps (approximately ¼ pound)
⅛ teaspoon salt

SAUCE
2 tablespoons butter
2 tablespoons finely chopped onion
1½ teaspoons curry powder
2 tablespoons flour
¾ cup light cream
Pinch of dried thyme
½ teaspoon salt

Place shrimps in a small saucepan and add cold water to cover. Over medium heat, bring the water to a simmer. Keep at a simmer over medium heat and cook, uncovered, for 4 to 6 minutes, or until the shrimps turn pink and are firm to the touch. Immediately drain them under cold running water to stop their cooking; keep under the running water until they are cool.

Shell and devein the shrimps. With a small sharp knife, cut them lengthwise into halves, then cut across into slices about ⅛ inch thick. Sprinkle the shrimp bits with salt, toss thoroughly, and set aside.

Preheat oven to 450° F.

SAUCE

Melt the butter in a small heavy saucepan over low heat. When the butter is hot, add the onion. Raise the heat to medium, and let onion cook for 2 to 3 minutes, or until bits are transparent. Stirring with a wooden spoon, add the curry powder to the onion, and continue to stir until mixture is well blended. Cook for 1 minute more, and *remove from the heat.* Add the flour, stirring it in with a wire whisk until all the ingredients are thoroughly blended.

Still stirring, return the pan to medium heat. Continuing to stir, cook the mixture for 2 minutes, then *remove from the heat.* Still using the wire whisk, beat constantly while gradually adding the cream, then the thyme and the salt.

Continuing to beat, return the pan to high heat and bring to a boil. Immediately, reduce the heat to low; no longer beating, let the sauce simmer for 4 minutes. *Remove from the heat.*

Place a strainer over a small bowl; using the back of a wooden spoon, push the sauce through. Stir the shrimps into the sauce until all the bits are evenly coated.

To fill and bake the ramekins

Fill each ramekin with 1 tablespoon of the shrimp mixture, mounding slightly. Arrange the ramekins on an ungreased small cookie sheet. Place on middle shelf of the oven, and bake for 5 minutes.

Remove from the oven. With a metal spatula, transfer the ramekins from the cookie sheet to a platter. Serve hot.

NOTES:
REFRIGERATOR STORAGE: Ramekins filled with curried shrimps are safely stored for up to 3 hours. Curried shrimps in a bowl, covered with plastic wrap, are safe for 1 day.
FREEZER STORAGE: Ramekins filled with curried shrimps can be safely frozen for up to 3 weeks if wrapped so as to be airtight. Transfer from freezer to preheated 450° F. oven and bake for 5 minutes.

CRABMEAT AU GRATIN

(MAKES FILLING FOR 12 RAMEKINS)

CRABMEAT
½ cup crabmeat (¼ pound), fresh, frozen, or canned

SAUCE
2 tablespoons unsalted butter
2 tablespoons finely chopped onion
2 tablespoons flour
¾ cup light cream
Pinch of dried thyme
½ teaspoon salt
Freshly ground black pepper
½ teaspoon Worcestershire sauce
1 egg yolk

TOPPING
½ cup freshly grated Swiss cheese
¼ cup freshly grated Parmesan cheese

Thoroughly drain crabmeat and carefully remove all the cartilage; place the crabmeat in a small bowl and set it aside.
Preheat oven to 450° F.

SAUCE

Melt the butter in a small heavy saucepan over low heat. When the butter is hot, add the onion. Raise the heat to medium, and let onion cook for 2 to 3 minutes, or until transparent, then *remove from the heat.* Add the flour, stirring it in with a wire whisk until ingredients are thoroughly blended.

Still stirring, return the pan to medium heat. Continuing to stir, cook the mixture for 2 minutes, then *remove from the heat.* Still using the wire whisk, beat constantly while gradually adding the cream, then the thyme, salt, pepper to taste, and Worcestershire sauce.

Continuing to beat, return the pan to high heat, and bring to a boil. Immediately reduce the heat to low. No longer beating, let the sauce simmer for 4 minutes. *Remove from the heat.*

Place a strainer over a small bowl; using a wooden spoon, push the sauce through. With a wire whisk, first beat the egg yolk lightly, then beat it into the strained sauce. Using a wooden spoon, stir the crabmeat into the sauce until all ingredients are well blended.

To fill and bake the ramekins

Distribute the sauced crabmeat evenly in the ramekins, mounding it slightly. Sprinkle the tops with the combined cheeses. Arrange the ramekins on an ungreased small cookie sheet. Place on the middle shelf of the oven, and bake for 5 minutes.

Remove from the oven. With a metal spatula, transfer the ramekins from the cookie sheet to a platter. Serve hot.

NOTES:

REFRIGERATOR STORAGE: Prebaked ramekins filled with crabmeat au gratin can be safely stored for up to 3 hours. Transfer from refrigerator to a preheated 450° F. oven. Bake for 5 minutes.

Sauced crabmeat in a bowl covered with plastic wrap is safely stored for 1 day.

BASIC TOMATO SAUCE and
FIVE PIZZA GARNISHES

(MAKES FILLING FOR 12 RAMEKINS)

BASIC TOMATO SAUCE

1 cup canned whole-packed tomatoes, drained; plus ½
    cup drained tomato liquid, reserved in a bowl
1 teaspoon tomato paste
1 tablespoon olive oil
2 tablespoons finely chopped onion
¼ teaspoon finely chopped garlic
¼ teaspoon dried orégano
¼ teaspoon sugar
¼ teaspoon salt
Pinch of freshly ground black pepper
2 tablespoons finely chopped parsley

Chop the tomatoes coarsely and add them to the reserved tomato liquid. Stir in the tomato paste, and set the mixture aside.

Place a 6- to 8-inch skillet over high heat, and pour in 1 tablespoon olive oil. When the oil is very hot, add the onion and immediately reduce the heat to medium. Stirring with a wooden
spoon, and shaking the pan from time to time, cook the onion for 2
minutes. Stir in the garlic, and cook until the onion is transparent.

Add the tomato mixture all at once. Stirring with a wooden
spoon, add the orégano, sugar, salt, pepper to taste, and parsley,
combining the ingredients well. Reduce the heat to low and
simmer, uncovered, for 20 minutes (set your timer).

Remove from heat, and set aside.

ക്ട«»ട്ര

PIZZA GARNISHES

Each recipe makes enough topping for 12 tomato-sauce-filled toast ramekins.

CHEESE PIZZA
½ cup freshly grated mozzarella cheese
¼ cup freshly grated Parmesan cheese

ANCHOVY PIZZA
6 flat anchovies, washed under cold running water,
    patted dry with paper towels, and cut into halves
½ cup freshly grated mozzarella cheese
¼ cup freshly grated Parmesan cheese

GREEN PEPPER AND ONION PIZZA
1 tablespoon olive oil
½ small onion, thinly sliced
½ small green pepper, cored, ribs removed, cut into
    thin strips
½ cup freshly grated mozzarella cheese
¼ cup freshly grated Parmesan cheese

Place a 6- to 8-inch skillet over high heat and pour in 1 tablespoon olive oil. When the oil is very hot, add the onion slices and pepper strips, and immediately reduce heat to low, stirring the onion and pepper with a wooden spoon. Cover and simmer for about 6 minutes, or until slightly underdone. Don't let them soften—they will continue to cook in the oven.

Remove from the heat. Uncover, and set aside.

SAUSAGE PIZZA
1½-inch piece of pepperoni, skinned, and cut into
    ¼-inch dice
½ cup freshly grated mozzarella cheese
¼ cup freshly grated Parmesan cheese

MUSHROOM PIZZA

1 tablespoon olive oil
4 medium-sized mushrooms, wiped clean with a damp
    cloth, and thinly sliced
Pinch of salt
Pinch of freshly ground black pepper
½ cup freshly grated mozzarella cheese
¼ cup freshly grated Parmesan cheese

Place a 6- to 8-inch skillet over high heat and pour in 1 tablespoon olive oil. When the oil is very hot, add the mushrooms and immediately reduce the heat to low. Add salt and pepper to taste. Stir once, cover, and cook for about 6 minutes, or until the mushrooms are soft.

Remove from the heat. Uncover, and set aside.

To fill, garnish, and bake the ramekins

Before filling and garnishing the ramekins, *allow at least 15 minutes to preheat oven to 450° F.*

Prepare the pizza garnish, and set it aside.

Spoon some of the tomato sauce into each of the 12 ramekins, distributing it evenly. Top each filled ramekin with some of the garnish. Distribute the garnish evenly (use your fingers), always ending with a sprinkling of mozzarella cheese and a more generous one of Parmesan cheese. Arrange the ramekins on an ungreased small cookie sheet. Place it on the middle shelf of the oven and bake for 5 minutes. Remove from the oven, and transfer the ramekins to a platter with a metal spatula. Serve hot.

NOTES:

To prepare ahead of time: Do *not* fill toast ramekins with tomato sauce before refrigerating; the sauce will saturate the ramekins. Refrigerate the sauce in a bowl covered with plastic wrap; it will keep safely for up to 3 days.

STORAGE: Prebaked ramekins can be stored safely in a plastic bag at room temperature or in the refrigerator for 3 days.

Garnishes can be made 1 day ahead of time. Refrigerate, covered with plastic wrap.

FREEZER STORAGE: Sauce and ramekins can be safely frozen separately for up to 3 months—the sauce in an airtight container, the ramekins wrapped carefully so as to be airtight. Defrost sauce in a pan on top of the stove over *very* low heat. Preheat oven to 450° F. Transfer sauce to frozen ramekins just before baking. Top with garnish, and bake for 5 minutes. Garnishes *cannot* be frozen.

Grated cheeses, refrigerated in plastic bags, will retain their freshness for 4 to 6 days.

SAUSAGE IN PASTRY

(SERVES 6 TO 8)

> 2 teaspoons softened butter
> 1 garlic-flavored sausage, 8 to 10 inches long and 2 to 2½
>   inches in diameter
> 3 tablespoons Dijon mustard
> 1 recipe Flaky Pastry (p. 25)
>
> *GLAZE*
> 1 egg
> 1 tablespoon milk or cream

With the 2 teaspoons softened butter, grease a small cookie sheet, and set it aside.

With the tip of a sharp knife, prick the skin of the sausage in 8 to 10 places, and put it into a 3- to 4-quart pot with water to cover. Bring the water to a boil over high heat. Turn the heat to simmer and cook, partially covered, for 45 minutes (set your timer). Drain the sausage and set it aside.

When the sausage is cool enough to handle, skin it with a small sharp knife.

Remove the chilled pastry from the refrigerator, unwrap, and place it on a lightly floured surface. Dust the top lightly with flour, and roll it out into an oval 6 × 12 inches and ⅛ inch thick. If the pastry sticks to the surface when you roll it, dust underneath lightly with flour.

To encase the sausage in the pastry, begin with the long sides of the pastry oval facing you horizontally. Spread the Dijon mustard over the entire sausage. Place the sausage so that it lies horizontally on the long edge of the pastry nearest you. Roll up the sausage in the pastry, making one complete turn to enclose it. Evenly *trim off all but 1 inch of the length of the pastry*; leave the side extensions untrimmed.

With a pastry brush dipped into water, dampen the 1-inch strip of pastry extending beyond the sausage. Fold the dampened strip back onto the pastry enclosing the sausage, and press to make it

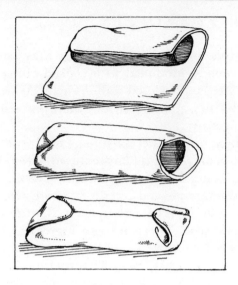

adhere. Roll the sausage over the seam to make it adhere more securely.

Turn the sausage so that the seam side faces you. Trim only the rough edges of the side flaps, fold them inward, and press the edges firmly to the seam.

Turn the sausage seam side down onto the buttered cookie sheet, and press again to make the flaps adhere more securely to the seam.

To decorate the top of the sausage, roll out the excess pastry and cut out decorative shapes with a cookie cutter. Dampen the underside of each shape with water and press them onto the pastry. Leave the sausage in place on the cookie sheet, and chill in the refrigerator for 15 minutes (set your timer).

Preheat oven to 375° F.

Just before baking the sausage, beat the egg and milk (or cream) together until well combined. With a pastry brush, paint a film of this mixture on top of the pastry. Place on the middle shelf of the oven and bake for 45 minutes (set your timer), or until the pastry is golden brown. Remove from the oven and transfer the sausage to a warm serving dish. Serve hot, cut into slices $\frac{1}{4}$ to $\frac{1}{2}$ inch thick, with additional mustard.

COCKTAIL TURNOVERS

Cocktail turnovers are made of rolled-out flaky pastry cut into 3- to 3½-inch rounds. Mounded with cooked filling, folded over and sealed, they resemble closed scallop shells. As neat to hold as one-bite morsels, they are, in fact, of "three-bite size," just right to savor and linger over.

There are three quite different fillings to choose from: subtle and mild Mushroom-Onion; creamy-textured, savory Blue Cheese; and one we call Coney Island—reminiscent of, but a far cry from, Hot Dog and Sauerkraut—and certain to be a conversation piece.

One recipe of a filling is enough to make 26 to 28 cocktail turnovers of the same type. There are two ingredient lists for flaky pastry; for Cocktail Turnovers, use the amounts for 1½ recipes, on page 26; these will make 26 to 28 turnovers. Remember that flaky pastry must chill for at least 1 hour before rolling it out. If you make the pastry ahead and freeze it, move it from the freezer to the refrigerator the night before.

The basic procedure for making cocktail turnovers is to select a filling, cook it, and set it aside before you roll out the pastry and cut it into rounds.

> 1 recipe selected filling
> 2 tablespoons softened butter
> 1½ recipes Flaky Pastry (p. 26), chilled for at least 1 hour
>
> *GLAZE*
> 1 egg
> 2 tablespoons cream or milk

Cook the filling you have selected and set it aside.

Lightly grease a cookie sheet 14 × 16 inches with 2 tablespoons softened butter. Set it aside.

Remove the pastry from the refrigerator, unwrap, and place it on a lightly floured surface. Lightly flour the top of the pastry and your rolling pin. Roll out the pastry into a circular shape. Always roll out from the center of the pastry, ending each stroke just short of the edge so as not to thin out the edge too soon; you need

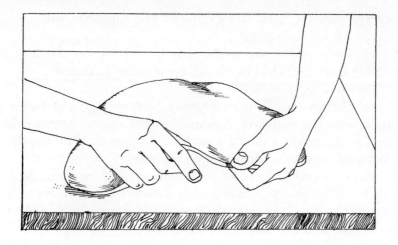

a little thickness to hold when you turn it. Never roll back toward the center. Turn the pastry clockwise from time to time to test if it is sticking to the surface. If it sticks, flour lightly underneath. Continue rolling it out until it is ⅛ inch thick, including the edge.

With a 3- to 3½-inch cookie cutter, press out rounds of pastry as close together as you can. Gather the scraps, quickly make them into a ball, press it into a cake with the flat of your hand, and roll it out again. Press out more rounds. Repeat the whole procedure until all the pastry is used. If your kitchen is too warm, your pastry may oversoften, making it difficult to press out all the rounds. If so, gather the scraps, shape into a ball, then a cake, wrap in wax paper, and chill in the refrigerator for a few minutes. While the scraps chill, you can begin to fill the first group of turnovers, but *be sure a hot filling has cooled to room temperature.*

On half of each round, place 1 generously mounded teaspoon of filling. Pat it down lightly, leaving ⅛-inch edge of pastry exposed. Dip the tip of a finger into cold water and moisten the edge of the entire round.

With your fingers, lift the uncovered half—if it sticks to the surface, slide a metal spatula underneath—and fold it over the filling so that the edges of the pastry meet evenly, and press the edges together. To secure the edges even more, press them together with the back of fork tines. The turnovers will now resemble closed scallop shells.

Place the turnovers, evenly spaced in rows, on the prepared cookie sheet, and chill in the refrigerator for 15 minutes.

Preheat oven to 425° F.

Just before baking the turnovers, beat the egg and cream (or milk) together until well combined. With a pastry brush, paint a film of the mixture on the top of each turnover. With the *tips* of fork tines, prick each turnover on top *once*.

Place the cookie sheet on the middle shelf of the oven and bake for 15 to 20 minutes, until golden. Remove from the oven. With a metal spatula, transfer the turnovers from the cookie sheet to a wire rack to cool slightly. Serve warm.

MUSHROOM-ONION FILLING

(MAKES FILLING FOR 26 TO 28 TURNOVERS)

> 2 tablespoons unsalted butter
> ½ cup finely chopped onion
> ½ teaspoon finely chopped garlic
> ½ pound fresh mushrooms, wiped clean with a paper
>   towel, and finely chopped
> 1 tablespoon all-purpose flour
> 2 tablespoons cream
> ½ teaspoon salt
> ¼ teaspoon freshly ground black pepper
> ¼ teaspoon dried thyme
> 2 tablespoons finely chopped parsley

Melt the butter in an 8- to 10-inch skillet over medium heat. When the butter is very hot (don't let it brown), add the onion and garlic. Stirring with a wooden spoon, and shaking the pan from time to time, cook for 4 to 6 minutes, or until the onion is transparent.

Add the mushrooms, cooking and stirring until the ingredients are well blended. Reduce heat to low, cover the pan, and allow to cook for 15 minutes. Uncover, and turn heat to high; stirring constantly, cook away all the liquid. *Remove from heat.*

One ingredient at a time, stir in the flour, cream, salt, pepper to taste, thyme, and chopped parsley. Continue stirring all the ingredients together to blend them thoroughly. Place the pan over low heat, and cook until the mixture thickens to a pastelike consistency. *Remove from heat,* transfer the filling to a bowl, and let cool to room temperature.

CONEY ISLAND FILLING

        3 all-beef frankfurters
        3 slices of lean bacon
        1/2 pound sauerkraut
        1/2 cup finely chopped onion
        1/2 cup chicken broth, homemade or canned
        1 hard-cooked chopped egg
        2 tablespoons chopped fresh dill, or 1 teaspoon dried
            dillweed
        1/4 teaspoon salt (depending on saltiness of the chicken
            broth)
        1/4 teaspoon freshly ground black pepper
        1 tablespoon prepared mustard

With a sharp knife cut the frankfurters into 1/4-inch dice, and set aside.

Cook the bacon over medium heat, and place on paper towels to drain. Measure 4 teaspoons of the bacon fat into an 8- to 10-inch skillet and set aside. (The rest of the bacon fat may be discarded or saved for another use.)

Place the sauerkraut in a colander and wash it under cold running water. Rearrange it with your hands from time to time so that the water gets to all of it and washes away its acidity. This should take about 4 minutes. Lift the sauerkraut from the colander with your hands, press the water out, and place the sauerkraut in a small bowl. Set aside.

Place the skillet with the bacon fat over medium heat. When the fat is hot, add the onion and cook until it is transparent. *Remove from heat.* Using a wooden spoon, stir in the sauerkraut until it is well blended with the onion.

Return the pan to medium heat and add the chicken broth all at once. Flatten the sauerkraut-onion mixture into the broth with a wooden spoon. Reduce heat to low, cover the pan, and cook for 15 minutes.

Remove the cover, and turn heat to high; stirring constantly to prevent scorching, reduce the liquid in the pan until the sauerkraut is dry. Check for residual liquid by tilting the pan and pressing the sauerkraut with a wooden spoon; if liquid flows out, continue to cook until the mixture sticks just slightly to the pan. *Remove from heat.* Immediately, transfer the sauerkraut to a bowl, stir in the diced frankfurters, and set aside.

Chop the bacon into fine pieces and add to the sauerkraut. Add the chopped egg and dill. Taste for salt. Add the freshly ground pepper, or more to taste, and the mustard; with a wooden spoon mix until all the ingredients are well blended. Taste once more for seasoning, and let cool to room temperature.

BLUE CHEESE FILLING

(MAKES FILLING FOR 26 TO 28 TURNOVERS)

> 4 ounces Danish blue cheese
> 4 ounces cream cheese
> 1 teaspoon prepared mustard
> 1 egg yolk

   Place all the ingredients in a small bowl. Using a wooden spoon, cream them together until thoroughly blended.

NOTES:

REFRIGERATOR STORAGE: If made ahead of time, fillings keep safely for 2 to 3 days. If made ahead of time, unbaked filled turnovers keep for 2 to 3 days. Do not prick tops. Do not glaze.

FREEZER STORAGE: Fillings keep safely for 3 to 4 weeks in airtight containers. Unbaked, filled turnovers keep safely for 3 to 4 weeks, if wrapped so as to be airtight. Do not prick tops. Do not glaze.

TO BAKE: From refrigerator or freezer, transfer unbaked, filled turnovers to a greased cookie sheet. Glaze tops, prick tops *once*, and bake in a preheated 425° F. oven for 15 to 20 minutes.

COUNTRY PÂTÉ

When planning a large dinner or cocktail party, Country Pâté is a good choice because it can be made ahead of time. As a first course for a dinner party, it may be served with Mock French Bread (p. 106). The pâté can be sliced thinly like cold cuts; for a cocktail party, it can be used to make narrow, finger-length canapés.

(SERVES 12 TO 14)

1 pound very fatty bacon, very thinly sliced
1 teaspoon softened butter
3 tablespoons butter
1 cup finely chopped onion
2 teaspoons finely chopped garlic
1 pound lean veal ⎫
1 pound lean pork ⎬ *ground together*
½ pound pork fat ⎭
2 eggs
2½ teaspoons salt
½ teaspoon freshly ground black pepper
¼ teaspoon ground allspice
½ teaspoon crumbled dried thyme
¼ cup Cognac
2 bay leaves

Preheat oven to 350° F.

Blanch the fatty bacon strips by dropping them into boiling water, then bringing the water to a boil again. Drain the strips immediately, and keep them under cold running water until they are cool enough to handle. One at a time, lay them out on paper towels so they do not overlap, and pat them dry on top with more paper towels.

With the 1 teaspoon softened butter, grease the whole interior of a pâté dish 4 × 10 inches and 2½ to 3 inches deep. Line the bottom of the dish with bacon strips, laying them out one by one the full length of the bottom of the dish, slightly overlapping the strips. Reserve 3 or 4 strips for the top of the pâté. Continue over-lapping the strips up the sides, patching short strips together by overlapping, then pressing them together to make them adhere. When the entire dish is lined, place it in the refrigerator to chill while you prepare the filling.

Melt the remaining 3 tablespoons butter in a 10- or 12-inch skillet over medium heat. When the butter is very hot, add the onion and cook for about 4 minutes. Add the garlic, and cook until the onion is transparent. Remove from heat, and set aside until the mixture is cool enough to handle.

Place the ground meat mixture in a large bowl. Add the eggs, salt, pepper to taste, allspice, thyme, Cognac, and the cooled onion-garlic mixture. Using your hands, mix the ingredients together until they are thoroughly blended.

Remove the lined pâté dish from the refrigerator; again using your hands, pack the meat mixture into it. Smooth the top of the mixture, and cover it with the remaining bacon strips, laid out one by one and slightly overlapping. Press the bay leaves lightly onto the bacon strips, about 4 inches apart. Cover the dish with a piece of aluminum foil slightly longer than the dish, and set the lid on top of the foil.

Bring a pot of water to a boil over high heat. When the water is boiling, set the pâté dish in a roasting pan. Pull out the lower middle shelf of the oven and place the roasting pan on it. Pour enough of the boiling water into the pan to come at least halfway up the sides of the pâté dish. Slide the shelf back into the oven and bake for 1½ hours (set your timer).

Remove the pâté dish from the roasting pan and let it rest, cov-ered, until it comes to room temperature. Remove the foil. Cover the dish with its lid, and refrigerate overnight. Serve cold.

NOTES:
To make finger-length canapés, slice the pâté thinly; place on lightly buttered bread of your choice and cut into narrow strips.
REFRIGERATOR STORAGE: Keeps safely for 3 to 4 days.
Although Country Pâté can be frozen safely, it becomes unpalatable in tex-ture, and loses some of its flavor.

FILLETS OF SOLE IN A TART SHELL

Fillets of Sole in a Tart Shell is in the style of the French classic fillets of sole Dugléré, but in a new guise. The adaptation consists of arranging oven-poached fillet cylinders to form a wheellike pattern in a prebaked tart shell, then masking them with sauce Dugléré. The tart is served hot from the oven. Presented on a circular serving platter, the tart is spectacular. At the serving table, cut it so that each fillet cylinder lies on its own wedge of pastry, then transfer each wedge to an individual plate. The guests invited "for drinks" are sure to remember this accompaniment. This dish can also be served as a main dish for lunch.

(SERVES 6)

FISH
3 fillets of sole, 8 ounces each
Salt
Freshly ground black pepper
2 tablespoons softened unsalted butter
1/4 cup chopped shallots
1/4 cup water
1/4 cup clam juice
1/2 cup white wine

SAUCE
3 tablespoons unsalted butter
4 teaspoons flour
1/2 cup heavy cream
Salt
Pinch of cayenne
2 large tomatoes, blanched and peeled, then seeded and
    cut into 1/4-inch strips
2 tablespoons chopped parsley
1 fully baked Tart Shell (p. 27), cooled to room
    temperature
1/4 cup freshly grated Parmesan cheese

Preheat oven to 370° F.

Wash fillets under cold running water, then pat dry with paper towels. With a sharp knife, cut each fillet down the center into 2 long, equal-sized pieces. Place each half fillet between 2 pieces of wax paper; using the broad side of a cleaver, flatten each one to ¼ inch in thickness. Peel off and discard the paper, then lightly salt and pepper each fillet on both sides. One at a time, starting at the narrowest end, roll up each one into a cylinder.

With the 2 tablespoons softened butter, grease a baking dish 7 × 12 inches. Scatter the chopped shallots into the dish, then lightly sprinkle them with salt and pepper. Lay out the rolled fillets in one layer, then sprinkle them again lightly with salt and pepper. Pour the water into the dish, then the clam juice and white wine. Cover the dish with buttered wax paper, buttered side down, and place on the middle shelf of the oven. Bake for 15 minutes (set your timer).

Test for doneness by inserting the tips of fork tines into the thickest part of one fillet. If the fish comes apart easily and looks opaque, all the fillets are done. If they are not done, cover and bake for a few minutes longer.

Remove the dish from the oven. Lay out a double thickness of paper towels; using a slotted spoon, transfer the fillets to the paper towels. Cover with another layer of paper towels and allow the fillets to drain. Pour the cooking liquid from the baking dish into a bowl or a measuring cup, and set it aside to use in the sauce.

Raise oven heat to 425° F.

SAUCE

Melt 2 tablespoons of the butter in a heavy 1-quart saucepan over low heat. Add the flour, stirring it in with a wooden spoon until the mixture is smooth, and allow it to cook for 2 to 3 minutes. *Remove from heat.*

Gradually add the reserved cooking liquid, beating it into the butter-flour mixture with a wire whisk. Bring to a boil over high heat. Immediately turn down heat and allow the sauce to simmer for about 5 minutes (set your timer).

Stir in the cream, then the salt and cayenne to taste. Stir in the tomato strips, then the parsley, and taste for seasoning. Remove the sauce from heat.

Assembling the tart

Spoon about one third of the sauce into the fully baked tart shell, spreading it evenly but gently over the entire bottom. Place the fillet cylinders on the sauce, spacing them evenly so that when served, each will lie on an equal-sized wedge of pastry. Spoon over the remaining sauce, then sprinkle with grated Parmesan cheese. With the remaining 1 tablespoon butter, dot the entire surface of the filling. Place on the middle shelf of the oven and bake for 10 minutes (set your timer). Serve hot.

BAKED SHELLFISH

(SERVES 4)

> 12 oysters, or 24 Little Neck Clams on the half shell
> 4 tablespoons butter
> 1 cup fresh bread crumbs (see Notes)
> ½ teaspoon finely chopped garlic
> 2 tablespoons finely chopped scallion
> 2 tablespoons chopped fresh Italian parsley
> Salt
> Freshly ground black pepper
> Lemon wedges

Preheat oven to 425° F.

Set each oyster or clam in its half shell on a dish, and set aside.

Melt the butter in a 10-inch skillet over medium heat. When the butter is very hot, add the bread crumbs; with a wooden spoon stir them constantly as they toast, darkening evenly, to pale gold, 4 to 6 minutes. Stir in the garlic. Alternate stirring the mixture and shaking the pan for about 1 minute. Stir in the scallion, then the parsley—just to heat them through—and remove from heat. Immediately, scrape the contents of the skillet into a bowl. (Doing this at once keeps the bread crumbs from overtoasting.)

Cover the top of each oyster or clam with some of the mixture, distributing all of it equally. Sprinkle each topping lightly with salt and a grinding of black pepper. Transfer the shellfish to a baking sheet large enough to hold them without crowding. Place the baking sheet on the middle shelf of the oven and bake for 10 minutes (set your timer).

Remove the baking sheet from the oven. With a metal spatula, transfer the shellfish to serving dishes. Serve hot, with lemon wedges.

NOTE:

To make fresh bread crumbs, use 3 slices of fresh white bread; remove crusts, and reduce bread to crumbs in a blender.

BAKED MUSSELS OR CLAMS, ITALIAN STYLE

The ingredient list calls for 30 mussels, or 2 dozen Little Neck clams on the half shell. The extra mussels are to be considered spares, so to speak, in case a few of the mussels do not open when steamed. There is enough sauce to top 24; if all should open, just distribute it a little less generously.

(SERVES 6)

> 30 mussels, or 2 dozen Little Neck clams on the half
>   shell
> ¼ pound (1 stick) unsalted butter, softened
> 2 tablespoons chopped scallion
> ½ teaspoon chopped garlic
> 2 tablespoons chopped fresh Italian parsley
> ½ teaspoon crumbled dried orégano
> ¼ teaspoon salt
> ¼ teaspoon freshly ground black pepper
> Lemon wedges

If you are using Little Neck clams, set them aside on their half shells. If you are using mussels, pull off their beards under cold running water, and scrub the shells well. Put ½ cup cold water into a large pot that has a tight-fitting cover. Add the mussels. Cover the pot, and bring the water to a boil over high heat. Turn the heat to simmer, and steam the mussels, covered, for 5 minutes. Discard any mussels that do not open.

Dump the mussels into a colander and let them stand until they are cool enough to handle.

Preheat oven to 450° F.

Using a wooden spoon, cream the butter with the scallion, garlic, parsley, orégano, salt and pepper to taste until all the ingredients are thoroughly blended.

Tear the top shell from each of the mussels and discard it. Arrange the mussels, each in its half shell, or each Little Neck clam in its half shell, in an ovenproof dish or on a jelly-roll pan.

Top each mussel or clam with a generous amount of the butter mixture. Place the dish or jelly-roll pan on the middle shelf of the oven. Bake for 5 minutes (set your timer).

Using a metal spatula, transfer the baked shellfish to serving dishes. Serve hot with lemon wedges.

Soups

GOLDEN CHICKEN BROTH

No commercially canned chicken broth will match the fresh, concentrated chicken flavor of this one, made of 5 pounds of necks and backs to 4 quarts of water. It is also ideal for any sauce requiring chicken broth, conveniently frozen in 1- or 2-cup quantities.

What accounts for its golden color is leaving the onion skin on; the natural pigment in the skin tints the liquid. Whether golden or pale, the actual flavor is the same; but a broth rich in color has the psychological effect of making it taste even richer. When served as a clear soup with a garniture, the golden color heightens its appeal.

The skin of yellow onions has long been used as a natural coloring agent, but as a culinary device, designed specifically for enhancing chicken soup, it is attributed to the Jewish kitchen. It is also the Jewish kitchen that provides Matzoh Balls—one of the most toothsome garnitures for Golden Chicken Broth. Interestingly enough, the most reliable directions for making them appear on any box of matzoh meal.

Any number of garnitures may be added to this broth: very fine egg noodles—available in most supermarkets; cooked, cubed fresh vegetables such as carrots and/or celery; a small amount of cooked rice. Whichever garniture you decide to use, first cook it separately, then reheat it in the soup. (Cooking it in the soup would cloud the golden color.) When serving, add ½ teaspoon of chopped fresh parsley to each plate of soup—a delicate aesthetic touch, but also flavorsome and nourishing.

(MAKES ABOUT 4 QUARTS)

> 5 pounds chicken backs and necks
> 4 quarts cold water
> 2 parsley sprigs
> 1 medium-sized carrot
> 3 medium-sized yellow onions, skin left on
> 3 celery ribs, leaves left on
> 1 tablespoon salt
> 1 teaspoon whole peppercorns
> 3 whole cloves
> 1 large bay leaf

Preheat oven to 400° F.

Wash the chicken backs and necks under cold running water. Place them in an 8- to 10-quart casserole that has a cover, add the water, and bring to a boil over high heat. Use a slotted spoon to skim off the foam that rises to the top. Remove from the heat.

Add the remaining ingredients, and immediately place the casserole on the lower shelf of the oven. Partially cover the casserole, and bake for 2 hours. (The casserole is partially covered to allow steam to escape so that condensation does not drip back into the broth.)

Remove the casserole from the oven. Set a fine-meshed sieve over a large heatproof bowl, and strain the contents of the casserole. Discard the solids that remain in the sieve. Let the broth come to room temperature before refrigerating or freezing.

NOTES:
REFRIGERATOR STORAGE: Safe for 3 to 4 days.
FREEZER STORAGE: Safe for 3 to 4 months, if stored in an airtight container.

BEEF BROTH

When you make this rich beef broth, it's a good idea to have for an entrée the fresh brisket called for in this recipe. Fresh brisket is an exceptionally flavorsome cut of meat. (If you have a piece left over, see Notes for interesting ways to use it.)

Served as a soup, the broth is delicious with any one of a number of garnitures such as fresh vegetables, rice, broad or fine noodles. Cook the garniture separately, and reheat it in the soup; leftover bits of brisket cut into dice make a fine addition.

The flavor of any sauce requiring beef broth will be enriched by this recipe.

(MAKES ABOUT 3 QUARTS)

> 2 to 2½ pounds fresh brisket, in 1 piece
> 5 pounds beef bones (meaty neck bones and
>   marrow bones, mixed)
> 4 quarts cold water
> 1 tablespoon salt
> 1 medium-sized carrot
> 1 medium-sized parsnip
> 3 celery ribs, leaves left on
> 1 teaspoon whole peppercorns
> ½ teaspoon dried thyme
> 1 large bay leaf
> 2 parsley sprigs

Preheat oven to 400° F.

Place the brisket and bones in an 8- to 10-quart casserole that has a cover. Add the water, and bring to a boil over high heat. Use a slotted spoon to skim off the foam that rises to the top. Remove from heat.

Add the remaining ingredients, and immediately place the casserole on the lower shelf of the oven. Partially cover the casserole, and bake for 2½ hours. (The casserole is partially covered to allow steam to escape so that condensation does not drip back into the broth.)

When the broth has baked for 2½ hours, transfer the brisket to a platter and reserve for later use (see Notes). Continue to bake the broth, partially covered, for 1 hour more (set your timer).

Remove the casserole from the oven. Strain the contents of the casserole through a fine-meshed sieve into a large heatproof bowl. Discard the solids that remain in the sieve. Let the broth come to room temperature before refrigerating or freezing.

NOTES:
Suggestions for leftover brisket in 1 piece:
Cooked brisket can be stored in refrigerator for 3 to 4 days when covered with plastic wrap.
1. Remove from the refrigerator and reheat it slowly in some of the broth. There is no loss of flavor or texture.
2. Cold, or at room temperature, leftover brisket is delicious sliced.
3. Cold, or at room temperature, brisket is excellent sliced and used for sandwiches.
4. Cold, cubed, and combined with cold, cubed cooked vegetables, this cut makes a delightful salad. Toss it lightly with an oil and vinegar dressing.

REFRIGERATOR STORAGE: Broth safe for 3 to 4 days.
FREEZER STORAGE: Broth safe for 3 to 4 months, if stored in airtight container. It is convenient to have this broth in 1-pint containers. When recipes call for the broth for use in a sauce, for example, it is simpler to defrost a small quantity.

LEEK AND POTATO SOUP

You can make this soup two ways—either country style, with the potato cubes left whole, or as smooth and elegant as its cousin, Vichyssoise. Either way you choose to make it, the great trio—leek, potato, and chicken broth—works in unison to give this soup a subtle lift in flavor.

(SERVES 6 TO 8)

> 4 leeks, each approximately 1½ inches in diameter
> 1½ pounds potatoes, peeled and cut into 1-inch cubes
> 1 cup finely chopped onion (1 large onion)
> 2 quarts chicken broth, homemade or canned
> ¼ teaspoon freshly ground white pepper
> ½ cup heavy cream
> 4 tablespoons unsalted butter, softened
> ¼ cup chopped chives, fresh or freeze-dried

Preheat oven to 400° F.
To handle a leek easily when washing and slicing it, its base must be kept intact. Use all of the white part and 1 inch of the green, none of the long leaves. Cut, wash, and slice the leeks.

How to prepare leeks

With a sharp paring knife, shave away the roots to expose the cylindrical bottom of the base. Pull off any bruised leaves and discard them. Place the leek on your chopping board so that it lies horizontally; leaving 1 inch of green part, cut off the leaves and discard them.

Insert the tip of your paring knife ½ inch above the base—cutting edge facing the green top of the leek. Holding the handle at an angle, plunge the knife all the way in, and slash straight through and up the green top.

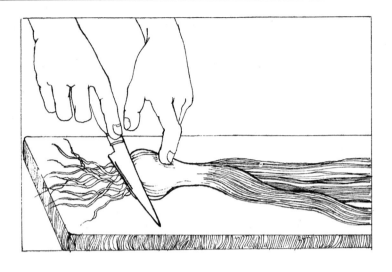

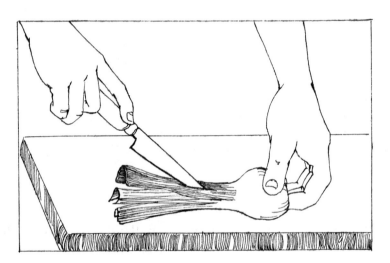

Hold the base of the leek in your hand like a knob, spread the layers apart under cold running water, and wash them thoroughly. Rub the layers clean on both sides and in between, to rid them of any dirt, sand, or grit. With paper towels, pat the layers dry, inside and out; set aside while you prepare remaining leeks. Lay them on your chopping board horizontally; one at a time, cut them into ⅛-inch slices; discard the tough cylindrical bottom.

In a 3- to 4-quart casserole that has a tight-fitting cover, place the leek slices, potatoes, onion, chicken broth, and white pepper. Uncovered, and over high heat, bring the contents of the casserole to a boil. Cover, and transfer the casserole to the middle shelf of the oven. Bake the soup for 45 minutes.

Remove the casserole from the oven. Ladle off 2 cups of the contents into the container of an electric blender and blend at high speed for about 30 seconds. Return the purée to the soup and stir it through. Stir in the cream, then the softened butter and the chives. Taste for salt and pepper. Cover the casserole, return it to the oven, and bake the soup for 15 minutes more.

For a uniformly smooth soup: Follow the recipe exactly as given through the 45-minute baking period, and remove the casserole from the oven. Transfer *all* the soup to a large bowl. In batches, purée all of it at high speed (about 30 seconds for each batch), and return each container of purée to the casserole. Carry out the rest of the recipe just as for country-style Leek and Potato Soup.

NOTES:

REFRIGERATOR STORAGE: Let soup come to room temperature before refrigerating. Keeps safely for up to 3 days. Reheat, thinned with chicken broth or cream, over low heat on top of the stove.

FREEZER STORAGE: Let soup come to room temperature before freezing. Can be frozen safely for 4 to 6 weeks in an airtight container.

LENTIL SOUP

(SERVES 8 TO 10)

> 1 pound dried lentils
> 2 thin slices of bacon
> 1 large leek, washed and cut into 1/8-inch slices (see pages
>   85 and 86)
> 1 cup finely chopped onion (1 large onion)
> 1 cup diced carrot (1 large or 2 small carrots)
> 1/2 cup chopped celery (1 rib)
> 1 bay leaf
> 2 1/2 quarts water or chicken broth, homemade or canned
> 1 tablespoon salt (only if water is used)
> 4 frankfurters, sliced into 1/8-inch rounds
> Freshly ground pepper

Preheat oven to 400° F.

Place the lentils in a colander and wash them under cold running water. Sift through them with your hands from time to time to be sure the water gets to all of them, and finally runs clear.

Place the lentils in a 3- to 4-quart casserole that has a tight-fitting cover. Cut the bacon into thin slivers and add to the lentils. Add the leek slices, onion, carrot, celery, bay leaf, and the cold water (or stock). Add salt if needed. Place the casserole over high heat and bring to a boil. Cover, and transfer to the middle shelf of the oven. Bake for 1 hour.

Add the frankfurter rounds; taste for salt and pepper. Cover, and bake for 15 minutes more.

NOTES:

REFRIGERATOR STORAGE: Let soup come to room temperature before refrigerating. Keeps safely for up to 1 week. To reheat, add broth or water to thin the soup, and cook over very low heat.

FREEZER STORAGE: Let soup come to room temperature before freezing. Can be frozen safely for 3 to 4 months in an airtight container.

BLACK BEAN SOUP

(SERVES 8 TO 10)

> 1 pound dried black turtle beans
> 3 tablespoons butter
> 1½ cups coarsely chopped onions
> 1 garlic clove, crushed with the flat side of a knife
> 2 medium-sized carrots, coarsely chopped
> ½ cup coarsely chopped celery (about 2 ribs, leaves
>   included)
> 4 smoked ham hocks, cracked with a cleaver
> 4 quarts chicken broth, homemade or canned
> 2 bay leaves and 4 cloves, wrapped in cheesecloth and
>   tied tightly
> ½ teaspoon freshly ground black pepper
> 4 hard-cooked eggs
> 1 lemon

Place the black beans in a large colander and wash them under cold running water until the water runs clear. Sift through them with your hands from time to time to be sure the water gets to all of them.

Place the beans in a 6- to 8-quart casserole that has a cover. Add enough water to cover the beans, bring to a boil over high heat, and continue boiling for 2 or 3 minutes. Turn off heat, cover the casserole, and let the beans soak, covered, for 1 hour at room temperature (set your timer).

Preheat oven to 400° F.

Pour the contents of the casserole into a colander and let all the water drain off. Wash and dry the casserole, then melt the butter in it over medium heat. When the butter is very hot, stir in the onions, garlic, carrots and celery, and cook until the onions are golden brown.

Still over medium heat, add the ham hocks and the drained beans. Immediately, pour the chicken broth over, then add the bay leaves and cloves. Add the pepper, or more if you prefer. Turn the heat to high and bring the broth to a boil. Remove from the heat, and place the casserole on the lower shelf of the oven. Partially cover the casserole, and bake for 1½ hours.

Test for doneness by inserting a fork into a ham hock; if the bone separates from the meat, the soup is done. If the bone still adheres to the meat, cover the casserole, bake for 10 to 15 minutes more, and test again.

Remove the casserole from the oven. Discard the ham hocks (or see Notes) and the cheesecloth bag of bay leaves and cloves. Set a food mill over a large mixing bowl and purée the soup mixture through it into the bowl. Purée the soup in batches, returning the puréed soup to the casserole.

Before serving, set the casserole over low heat until the soup is piping hot. Meanwhile, chop the hard-cooked eggs, and slice the lemon thinly. Garnish each serving with chopped eggs and a lemon slice. Pass a cruet of red-wine vinegar.

NOTES:

If you like to use the ham hocks, cut away all the fat, dice the meat, and add it to the soup.

REFRIGERATOR STORAGE: Let soup come to room temperature before refrigerating. Safe for 3 to 4 days. To reheat, thin with broth or water and cook over very low heat.

FREEZER STORAGE: Let soup come to room temperature before freezing. Keeps safely for 3 to 4 months in airtight containers.

GREEN SPLIT PEA SOUP

If you happen to have a ham bone with about 1 to 1½ cups of ham bits from it, use the bone and bits in place of the 1-pound ham steak called for in the ingredient list.

Split pea soup is a good old standby in almost every cook's repertoire, but this one combines with Cheese Bread (p. 112) as no other version of pea soup does with any other bread. If the weather is cold, the kitchen warm, serve Green Split Pea Soup with toasted Cheese Bread; it's a bracing food experience. And be sure to invite guests.

(SERVES 8 TO 10)

> 1 pound green split peas
> 3 tablespoons butter
> 1 cup finely chopped onion
> 1 celery rib, finely chopped
> 1 garlic clove, finely chopped
> 1 pound ham steak, diced
> 1 medium-sized carrot, grated
> 3 quarts chicken broth, homemade or canned
> 1 bay leaf
> ¼ teaspoon ground mace
> ½ teaspoon freshly ground black pepper

Preheat oven to 400° F.

Place the split peas in a wire strainer and wash them under cold running water until the water runs clear. Sift through them with your hands from time to time to be sure the water gets to all of them.

Over medium heat, melt the butter in a heavy 4- to 6-quart casserole that has a cover. When the butter is very hot, stir in the onion, celery, and garlic, and cook until the onion is transparent. Add the diced ham, grated carrot, and drained split peas. Pour the chicken broth over, then add the bay leaf, mace, and pepper, or use more pepper if you prefer. Turn heat to high and bring the broth to a boil.

Remove from the heat. Immediately, place the casserole on the lower shelf of the oven. Partially cover the casserole, and bake for 1 hour (set your timer).

NOTES:

REFRIGERATOR STORAGE: Let soup come to room temperature before refrigerating. Keeps safely for 3 to 4 days. To reheat, thin with water or broth over very low heat.

FREEZER STORAGE: Let soup come to room temperature before freezing. Keeps safely for 3 to 4 months if stored in an airtight container.

MUSHROOM BARLEY SOUP

(SERVES 8 TO 10)

    3 tablespoons unsalted butter
    ½ pound mushrooms, finely chopped
    1 cup finely chopped onion
    ¼ cup finely chopped carrot
    ¼ cup finely chopped celery
    1 pound whole-packed canned tomatoes, drained of
        liquid, then coarsely chopped
    ½ cup medium pearled barley
    3 quarts chicken or beef broth, homemade or canned
    Salt and pepper
    2 tablespoons finely chopped fresh parsley

Preheat oven to 400° F.

Over medium heat, melt the butter in a 4- to 6-quart casserole that has a cover. When the butter is very hot, stir in the mushrooms, reduce the heat to low, and cook until the mushrooms are soft.

Stir in the onion, carrot, and celery, and cook until the vegetables are lightly colored.

Stir in the tomatoes and barley. Add the broth, turn heat to high, and bring the broth to a boil. Remove from heat. Immediately, place the casserole on the lower shelf of the oven. Partially cover the casserole, and bake for 1 hour and 15 minutes, or until the barley is tender.

Remove the casserole from the oven. Add salt and pepper to taste. Just before serving, stir in the chopped parsley.

NOTES:
REFRIGERATOR STORAGE: Let soup come to room temperature before refrigerating. Keeps safely for 3 to 4 days.
FREEZER STORAGE: Let soup come to room temperature before freezing. Keeps safely for 3 to 4 months, if stored in an airtight container.

GOULASH SOUP

Goulash Soup is a nourishing one-dish meal that can be served in several different ways: thickened or unthickened, and with or without the addition of dumplings. If you plan to add dumplings, begin to prepare the batter about 15 minutes before the soup is done.

(SERVES 6 TO 8)

> 2 pounds beef chuck, trimmed of all fat, and cut into
>   ½-inch cubes
> ½ teaspoon caraway seeds
> 2 tablespoons imported sweet paprika
> 1 teaspoon finely chopped garlic (1 medium-sized clove)
> 1½ cups chopped onions
> 2 quarts cold water or chicken broth, homemade or
>   canned
> 1 tablespoon salt (only if water is used)
> ½ pound potatoes, cut into 1-inch cubes
> 1 large bell pepper, diced
> 4 carrots, scraped and thinly sliced
> 1 cup tomatoes (1-pound can, drained of all liquid)
> Freshly ground pepper

UNTHICKENED GOULASH SOUP

Preheat oven to 400° F.

Place the meat cubes in a 3- to 4-quart casserole that has a tight-fitting cover.

Wrap the caraway seeds in the corner of a kitchen towel; with the flat side of a cleaver, bang them a few times to crush them. Sprinkle the crushed seeds over the meat; add the paprika, garlic, and onions. Pour the water or broth over the ingredients. If you use water, add the salt. Remove the foam with a slotted spoon.

Place the casserole, uncovered, over high heat, and bring to a boil. Cover the casserole and transfer it to the lower middle shelf of the oven. Bake the soup for 1 hour.

Add the potato cubes and continue to bake the soup for 30 minutes. Add the diced pepper, the carrots and tomatoes, and bake the soup for 30 minutes longer. Taste for salt and pepper. Serve very hot.

THICKENED GOULASH SOUP

Follow the recipe through to the end, then remove the casserole from the oven to the top of the stove and keep it over low heat. Ladle a little of the soup liquid into the container of an electric blender; using a slotted spoon, add about half of the potato cubes. Purée the mixture at high speed for about 30 seconds. Stir the purée back into the soup.

THICKENED OR UNTHICKENED GOULASH SOUP WITH DUMPLINGS

Prepare the dumpling batter 15 minutes before the soup is done.

> ½ cup all-purpose flour
> 3 eggs
> ⅛ teaspoon salt

Combine the flour, eggs, and salt in a small bowl, and beat with a wooden spoon until the mixture is smooth, about 3 minutes.

Remove the casserole from the oven to the top of the stove and keep over low heat. Using a ½-teaspoon metal measuring spoon, drop the dumpling batter into the soup, 1 spoonful at a time. Cover the casserole, return to the middle shelf of the oven, and bake for 5 minutes.

NOTES:
REFRIGERATOR STORAGE: Let soup come to room temperature before refrigerating. Will keep safely for 3 to 4 days.
FREEZER STORAGE: Let soup come to room temperature before freezing. Will keep safely for 2 to 3 months in an airtight container.

Breads

WHITE BREAD

Compared with commercial white bread, this one is smoother and more tightly textured. You will find it perfect for sandwiches; it slices neatly and thinly and even straight from the freezer makes delicious toast.

(MAKES 1 LOAF)

> 1 package (¼ ounce) active dry yeast
> ½ cup warm water (110° to 115° F.)
> ½ teaspoon sugar
> 3 cups all-purpose flour
> 1 tablespoon salt
> 4 tablespoons unsalted butter, softened
> ¾ cup milk, first scalded then cooled to 110° to 115° F.
> Additional flour as needed
> 1 teaspoon softened butter
> 2 teaspoons softened butter

GLAZE
1 egg
2 teaspoons cream or milk

Add the yeast to the warm water, then add the sugar; using a fork, stir the ingredients together a few times. With a finger, wipe down into the mixture any yeast granules clinging to the tines of the fork. Set the mixture aside; the yeast will soon begin to foam slowly and increase in volume.

Place the flour and salt in a large mixing bowl; using a wooden spoon, combine the ingredients well. Place the 4 tablespoons softened butter on the flour. Pour in ¾ cup milk all at once, then the yeast mixture. Again using a wooden spoon, stir all the ingredients together (scrape in and include any bits adhering to the sides of the bowl) until the flour has absorbed all the liquid. Using your hands, gather the dough and shape it into a ball.

Lightly flour your work surface, place the ball of dough on it,

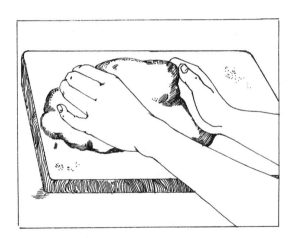

and knead it thoroughly for 10 minutes. Knead it in any way most comfortable for you, but knead it well—folding it forward, backward, bringing it in from the sides. Because of differences in the moisture of flour from bag to bag, the dough may stick to the work surface when you first knead it. Add flour underneath if it sticks and continue to add flour if it goes on sticking but only when you need it, and a little at a time. When the dough is shiny, smooth, and silky to your touch, shape it into a ball.

With the 1 teaspoon softened butter, grease the whole inside of a large clean mixing bowl. Roll the ball of dough about in the bowl to coat the entire surface with butter, and cover the bowl with a towel. Let the dough rise for 45 minutes (set your timer). **1st rise**

When the timer bell rings, the dough should be doubled in volume. To test it to see if it has risen enough, press 2 fingertips into the dough. If the indentations remain, it has risen enough. If they fill up and disappear, let the dough go on rising, testing this way until the indentations remain. Replace the towel between testings. When the dough has risen enough, punch it down once, and knead it in the bowl for 2 minutes. Replace the towel, and let the dough rise again for 30 minues (set your timer). **2nd rise**

With the 2 teaspoons softened butter, grease the whole inside of a bread pan 9 × 5 × 3 inches.

When the dough meets the indentation test, punch it down once more, and knead it in the bowl for 2 minutes. Flour your work surface lightly, place the dough on it, shape it into a loaf, and place it in the bread pan, pushing the dough into the corners of the pan. Cover the pan with the towel, and let the dough rise for 20 to 30 minutes (set your timer), or until the center of the loaf reaches the top of the pan. **3rd rise**

Double the ingredients for 2 loaves. If you make enough dough for 2 loaves, place the twice-risen dough on the work surface. Shape into 2 loaves and proceed as described for 1 loaf.

Preheat oven to 375° F.

Just before baking the bread, make the glaze by beating the egg and cream (or milk) together until well combined. Using a pastry brush, paint a film of the mixture on top of the loaf. Place the pan on the middle shelf of the oven, and bake for 45 minutes (set your timer).

Test for doneness by removing bread from pan onto a wire rack and rapping the bread with your knuckles; if it sounds hollow the bread is done; if not, return to pan and let it bake a little longer until it does. Turn the bread out of the pan, and cool it on a wire rack—top side up—to room temperature before cutting or storing.

NOTES:

REFRIGERATOR STORAGE: Wrapped in a plastic bag, keeps safely for 3 to 4 days.

FREEZER STORAGE: Keeps safely for 3 to 4 months, if carefully wrapped so as to be airtight. Defrost at room temperature for 1½ hours. Toast partially defrosted as soon as it can be sliced.

WHOLE WHEAT BREAD

The ingredient list tells the nutritional value of Whole Wheat Bread. What it doesn't tell is that it makes excellent sandwiches. One particular sandwich is always a great success. Surprisingly, it is one made with simple egg salad. Perhaps the secret of the successful combination is John Clancy's Egg Salad. If you would like to try it, see Notes.

(MAKES 1 LOAF)

> 2 packages (1/4 ounce each) active dry yeast
> 1/2 cup warm water (110° to 115° F.)
> 1/2 teaspoon sugar
> 2 1/2 cups stone-ground 100% whole-wheat flour
> 1 1/2 cups all-purpose flour
> 4 teaspoons salt
> 1 1/4 cups milk, first scalded, then cooled to
>   approximately 110° to 115° F.
> 1/4 cup unsulfured molasses
> Additional all-purpose flour as needed
> 1 teaspoon softened butter
> 2 teaspoons softened butter
>
> *GLAZE*
> 1 egg
> 2 tablespoons cream or milk

Add the yeast to the warm water, then the sugar; using a fork, stir the ingredients together a few times. With a finger, wipe down into the mixture any yeast granules clinging to the fork. Set the mixture aside; the yeast will soon begin to foam slowly and increase in volume.

Place the whole-wheat flour in a large mixing bowl, then the all-purpose flour and the salt; using a wooden spoon, combine the ingredients until they are thoroughly blended.

Pour in 1 1/4 cups of milk all at once. Add the molasses, using a rubber spatula to scrape all of it from the measuring cup. Add the yeast mixture. Again using a wooden spoon, stir all the ingredients together (scrape in and include any bits adhering to the sides of the bowl) until the flour has absorbed all the liquid. Using your hands, gather the dough and shape it into a ball.

Lightly flour your work surface, place the ball of dough on it, and knead it thoroughly for 10 minutes. Knead it in any way which is most comfortable for you, but knead it well—folding it forward, backward, bringing it in from the sides. Because of differences in the moisture of flour from bag to bag, the dough may stick to the work surface when you first knead it. Add a little all-purpose flour underneath if it sticks and continue to add flour if it goes on sticking but only when you need it, and only a little at a time. When the dough is shiny, smooth, and silky to your touch, shape it into a ball.

With the 1 teaspoon softened butter, grease the whole inside of a large clean mixing bowl. Roll the ball of dough about in the bowl to coat the entire surface with butter. Cover the bowl with a towel. Let the dough rise for 1½ hours (set your timer).   **1st rise**

When the timer bell rings, the dough should be doubled in volume. To test it to see if it has risen enough, press 2 fingertips into the dough. If the indentations remain, it has risen enough. If they fill up and disappear, let the dough go on rising, testing this way until the indentations remain. Replace the towel between testings. When the dough has risen enough, punch it down once, and knead it in the bowl for 2 minutes. Replace the towel, and let the dough rise for another 1½ hours (set your timer).   **2nd rise**

With the 2 teaspoons softened butter, grease the whole inside of a bread pan 9 × 5 × 3 inches.

When the dough meets the indentation test, punch it down once more, and knead it in the bowl for 2 minutes. Flour your work surface lightly, place the dough on it, shape it into a loaf, and place it in the bread pan, pushing the dough into the corners of the pan. Cover the pan with the towel, and let the dough rise for 45 minutes (set your timer), or until the center of the loaf reaches the top of the pan.   **3rd rise**

Double the ingredients for 2 loaves. If you make enough dough for 2 loaves, place the twice-risen dough on the work surface and give it the karate chop. Shape into 2 loaves and proceed as described for 1 loaf.

Preheat oven to 375° F.

Just before baking the bread, make the glaze by beating the egg and cream (or milk) together until well combined. Using a pastry brush, paint a film of the mixture on top of the loaf. Place the pan on the middle shelf of the oven, and bake for 45 minutes (set your timer).

Test for doneness by removing bread from pan onto a wire rack and rapping the bread with your knuckles; if it sounds hollow the bread is done; if not, return to pan and let it bake a little longer. Turn the bread out of the pan and cool it on a wire rack—top side up—to room temperature before cutting or storing.

NOTES:

REFRIGERATOR STORAGE: Wrapped in a plastic bag, keeps safely for 2 to 3 days.

FREEZER STORAGE: Keeps safely for 2 to 3 months if carefully wrapped so as to be airtight. Defrost at room temperature for 1½ hours. Toast partially defrosted as soon as it can be sliced.

JOHN CLANCY'S EGG SALAD: Place the following ingredients in a small mixing bowl: 2 hard-cooked eggs, finely chopped; 2 tablespoons finely chopped parsley; 1 tablespoon finely chopped green pepper; 2 tablespoons chopped chives; ½ teaspoon prepared mustard. Add enough mayonnaise (preferably unsweetened), 3 to 4 tablespoons, to bind mixture. Add salt and pepper to taste. Using a wooden spoon, combine all the ingredients thoroughly. Refrigerate for 1 hour before using. Makes enough for 2 generous sandwiches.

MOCK FRENCH BREAD

Unlike supermarket "French Breads," often so soft they can be bent into a ring, this version has a hard crust more characteristic of true French bread. Like the true French dough, it contains no fat and therefore stales quickly. It is best served within an hour after removing from the oven.

(MAKES 2 LOAVES, EACH 15 INCHES LONG)

1 package (1/4 ounce) active dry yeast
1 1/2 cups warm water (110° to 115° F.)
1/2 teaspoon sugar
4 cups all-purpose flour
1 tablespoon salt
Additional flour as needed
2 teaspoons softened butter
1/2 cup yellow cornmeal

WASH
2 teaspoons salt
1/4 cup cold water

Add the yeast to the water, then the sugar; using a fork, stir the ingredients together a few times. With your finger, wipe down into the mixture any yeast granules clinging to the tines of the fork. Set the mixture aside; the yeast will soon begin to foam slowly and increase in volume.

Place 4 cups of flour and the salt in a large mixing bowl; using a wooden spoon, combine the ingredients well. Add the yeast mixture all at once. Again using a wooden spoon, stir all the ingredients together (scrape in and include any bits adhering to the sides of the bowl) until the flour has absorbed all the liquid. Using your hands, gather the dough and shape it into a ball.

Lightly flour your work surface, place the ball of dough on it, and knead it thoroughly for 10 minutes. Knead it in any way most comfortable for you, but knead it well—folding it forward, backward, bringing it in from the sides. If it sticks to the work surface, dust underneath lightly with flour. If it goes on sticking, add flour but only as you need it, and only a little at a time. When the dough is shiny, smooth, and silky to your touch, shape it into a ball. With the 2 teaspoons softened butter, grease the whole inside of a large clean mixing bowl. Roll the ball of dough about in it to coat the entire surface with butter, and cover the bowl with a towel. Let the dough rise for 60 minutes (set your timer).   **1st rise**

When the timer bell rings, the dough should be doubled in volume. To test to see if it has risen enough, press 2 fingertips into the dough. If the indentations remain, it has risen enough. If they fill up and disappear, let the dough go on rising, testing this way until the indentations remain. Replace the towel between testings. When the dough has risen enough, punch it down once, and knead it in the bowl for 2 minutes. Replace the towel, and let the dough rise for 45 minutes (set your timer).   **2nd rise**

Coat the entire surface of a large cookie sheet with the ½ cup of yellow cornmeal. Set the cookie sheet aside.

When the dough meets the indentation test, punch it down once more, and knead it in the bowl for 2 minutes. Flour your work surface lightly and place the dough on it. Aim for the center and give it the karate chop. Shape each piece of dough into a tapered loaf, 15 inches long and about 2 inches in diameter at the center. Transfer the loaves to the cornmeal-coated cookie sheet, setting them about 2 inches apart. With a single-edged razor blade, make 4 or 5 diagonal slashes on top of the loaf, 2 inches apart and about ½ inch deep. Cover the loaves with a towel and let the dough rise for 30 minutes (set your timer).   **3rd rise**

Preheat oven to 400° F.

Just before placing the loaves in the oven, bring a roasting pan of water to a boil. Meanwhile, dissolve 2 teaspoons salt in ¼ cup water. Dip a pastry brush into this wash and paint a film of it on the top of each loaf.

Center the pan of boiling water on the floor of the oven. Immediately place the cookie sheet with the loaves of dough on the middle shelf, and bake for 15 minutes (set your timer). Reduce heat to 350° F. and bake for 20 minutes more (set your timer). Test for doneness by rapping the bread with your knuckles. If it sounds hollow and the surface is crisp, the bread is done. If not, let it bake a little longer, and test again. Remove the loaves to wire racks, top side up. Cool to room temperature before cutting or storing.

NOTES:

FREEZER STORAGE: Keeps safely for 3 to 4 months, if carefully wrapped so as to be airtight. To serve, remove from freezer, unwrap, place on a cookie sheet, and heat in a slow oven for about 10 to 12 minutes, or until defrosted.

CARAWAY RYE BREAD

(MAKES 1 LOAF)

> 1 package (¼ ounce) active dry yeast
> ¼ cup warm water (110° to 115° F.)
> ½ teaspoon sugar
> 2 cups stone-ground rye flour
> 2 cups all-purpose flour
> 2 teaspoons salt
> ¾ cup milk, first scalded, then cooled to room
>   temperature
> ¼ cup unsulfured dark molasses
> 2 teaspoons caraway seeds
> Additional all-purpose flour as needed
> 1 teaspoon softened butter
> ½ cup yellow cornmeal
>
> *GLAZE*
> 1 egg white
> 1 tablespoon cold water
> 1 tablespoon caraway seeds

Add the yeast to the warm water, then the sugar; using a fork, stir the ingredients together a few times. With a finger, wipe down into the mixture any yeast granules still clinging to the tines of the fork. Set the mixture aside; the yeast will soon begin to foam and increase in volume.

Place the rye flour in a large mixing bowl, then the all-purpose flour and the salt; using a wooden spoon, combine the ingredients until they are thoroughly blended.

Pour in the milk all at once. Add the molasses, using a rubber spatula to scrape all of it from the measuring cup. Add the yeast mixture, then the 2 teaspoons caraway seeds. Again using a wooden spoon, stir all the ingredients together (scrape in and include any bits adhering to the sides of the bowl) until the flour has absorbed all the liquid. Using your hands, gather the dough and shape it into a ball.

Lightly flour your work surface, place the ball of dough on it, and knead it thoroughly for 10 minutes. Knead it in any way most comfortable for you, but knead it well—folding it forward, backward, bringing it in from the sides. If the dough sticks to the work surface, dust lightly underneath with flour, but use only all-purpose flour. If it goes on sticking, add flour but only as you need it, and only a little at a time. When the dough is shiny, smooth, and silky to your touch, shape it into a ball.

With the 1 teaspoon softened butter, grease the whole inside of a large clean mixing bowl. Roll the ball of dough about in it to coat the entire surface with butter. Cover the bowl with a towel. Let the dough rise for 1 hour and 15 minutes (set your timer). **1st rise**

When the timer bell rings, the dough should be doubled in volume. To test to see if it has risen enough, press 2 fingertips into the dough. If the indentations remain, it has risen enough. If they fill up and disappear, let the dough go on rising, testing this way until the indentations remain. Replace the towel between testings. When the dough has risen enough, punch it down once, and knead it in the bowl for 2 minutes. Replace the towel, and let the dough rise for 45 minutes (set your timer).   **2nd rise**

Coat the entire surface of a large cookie sheet with the ½ cup of yellow cornmeal, and set the cookie sheet aside.

When the dough meets the indentation test, punch it down once more, and knead it in the bowl for 2 minutes. Flour your work surface lightly, place the dough on it, and shape it into a round loaf. Transfer the loaf to the cornmeal-covered cookie sheet. Cover it with the towel, and let the dough rise for 45 minutes (set your timer).   **3rd rise**

Double the ingredients for 2 loaves. If you make enough dough for 2 loaves, place the twice-risen dough on the work surface and give it the karate chop. Shape into 2 loaves and proceed as described for 1 loaf.

Preheat oven to 375° F., 15 minutes before the end of the last rising.

Just before baking the bread, beat the egg white with 1 tablespoon water until well combined. Using a pastry brush, paint a film of this glaze on the top of the bread. Scatter the 1 tablespoon caraway seeds on the glaze. Place the cookie sheet on the middle shelf of the oven and bake for 35 to 45 minutes (set your timer).

Test for doneness by rapping your knuckles on the bread. If it sounds hollow and is a deep brown, the bread is done. If not, bake a little longer and test again.

Transfer the bread to a wire rack and cool, top side up, to room temperature before cutting or storing.

NOTES:

REFRIGERATOR STORAGE: Keeps safely for 4 to 6 days, if wrapped in a plastic bag.

FREEZER STORAGE: Keeps safely for 3 to 4 months, if wrapped so as to be air-tight. Defrost at room temperature for 1½ hours. Toast partially defrosted as soon as it can be sliced.

CHEESE BREAD

The color of Cheese Bread is as yellow as the yolk of a hard-cooked egg. As for its flavor, the Cheddar cheese and cayenne give it "bite." A tightly textured bread, it can be sliced thinly and makes a piquant-tasting toast.

(MAKES 1 LOAF)

> 2 packages (¼ ounce each) active dry yeast
> ¼ cup warm water (110° to 115° F.)
> ½ teaspoon sugar
> 4 cups all-purpose flour
> 1½ teaspoons salt
> ¼ teaspoon cayenne pepper
> 1 cup milk, first scalded, then cooled to 110° to 115° F.
> 3 eggs
> 1½ cups grated sharp Cheddar cheese
> Additional flour as needed
> 1 teaspoon softened butter
> 2 teaspoons softened butter
>
> *GLAZE*
> 1 egg
> 2 teaspoons cream or milk

Add the yeast to the warm water, then add the sugar; using a fork, stir the ingredients together a few times. With your finger, wipe down into the mixture any yeast granules clinging to the tines of the fork. Set the mixture aside; the yeast will soon begin to foam and increase in volume.

Place the flour in a large mixing bowl, and add the salt and the cayenne pepper; using a wooden spoon, combine the ingredients well. Pour in the cup of milk all at once, then the yeast mixture. Add the eggs and grated cheese; again using the wooden spoon, stir all the ingredients together (scrape in and include any bits adhering to the sides of the bowl) until the flour has absorbed all the liquid. Using your hands, gather the dough and shape it into a ball.

Lightly flour your work surface, place the ball of dough on it, and knead it thoroughly for 10 minutes. Knead it in any way most comfortable for you, but knead it well—folding it forward, backward, bringing it in from the sides. Because of differences in the moisture of flour from bag to bag, the dough may stick to the work surface when you first knead it. Add flour underneath if it sticks and continue to add flour if it goes on sticking but only when you need it, and a little at a time. When the dough is shiny, smooth, and silky to your touch, shape it into a ball.

With the 1 teaspoon softened butter, grease the whole inside of a large clean mixing bowl. Roll the ball of dough about in the bowl to coat the entire surface with butter, and cover the bowl with a towel. Let the dough rise for 1 hour and 15 minutes (set your timer). **1st rise**

When the timer bell rings, the dough should be doubled in volume. To test if it has risen enough, press 2 fingertips into the dough. If the indentations remain, it has risen enough. If they fill up and disappear, let the dough go on rising, testing this way until the indentations remain. Replace the towel between testings. When the dough has risen enough, punch it down once, and knead it in the bowl for 2 minutes. Replace the towel, and let the dough rise for 1 hour (set your timer). **2nd rise**

With the 2 teaspoons softened butter, grease the whole inside of a bread pan 9 × 5 × 3 inches.

When the dough meets the indentation test, punch it down once more, and knead it in the bowl for 2 minutes. Flour your work surface lightly, place the dough on it, shape it into a loaf, and place it in the bread pan, pushing the dough into the corners of the pan. Cover the pan with the towel, and let the dough rise for 45 minutes (set your timer), or until the center of the loaf reaches the top of the pan. **3rd rise**

Double the ingredients for 2 loaves. If you make enough dough for 2 loaves, place the twice-risen dough on the work surface and give it the karate chop. (See p. 5.) Shape into 2 loaves and proceed as described for 1 loaf.

Preheat oven to 375° F.

Just before baking the bread, make the glaze by beating the egg and cream (or milk) together until well combined. Using a pastry brush, paint a film of the mixture on top of the loaf. Place the pan on the middle shelf of the oven, and bake for 45 minutes (set your timer).

Test for doneness by removing bread from pan onto a wire rack and rapping the bread with your knuckles; if it sounds hollow the bread is done; if not, return to pan and let it bake a little longer until it does. Turn the bread out of the pan, and cool it on a wire rack—top side up—to room temperature before cutting or storing.

NOTES:

REFRIGERATOR STORAGE: Wrapped in a plastic bag, keeps safely for 3 to 4 days.

FREEZER STORAGE: Keeps safely for 3 to 4 months, if carefully wrapped so as to be airtight. Defrost at room temperature for 1½ hours. Toast partially defrosted as soon as it can be sliced.

IRISH SODA BREAD

If you are pressed for time but want a fresh homemade bread, Irish Soda Bread is the answer; it takes less than an hour to make from start to finish. As with all quick breads, it stales quickly; but Irish Soda Bread 1 or 2 days old makes marvelous toast.

(MAKES 1 LOAF)

> 4 cups all-purpose flour
> 2 teaspoons salt
> 1 teaspoon baking soda
> 2 tablespoons softened unsalted butter
> 1½ cups buttermilk or sweet milk
> 1 tablespoon softened unsalted butter
> 1 tablespoon all-purpose flour

Preheat oven to 375° F.

Sift 4 cups flour, the salt, and baking soda into a large mixing bowl. Add the 2 tablespoons softened butter; using your fingers, combine it with the flour until no butter spots show. Add the buttermilk or sweet milk; using a wooden spoon, beat the mixture (scrape in and include any bits adhering to the sides of the bowl) until it forms a mass. Remove the dough from the bowl, and with your hands shape it into a ball.

With the 1 tablespoon softened butter, grease a cookie sheet. Center the ball of dough on it. With a sharp knife make a criss-cross cut ½ to ¾ inch deep into the top of the dough. Sprinkle the 1 tablespoon flour over the top, and place on the middle shelf of the oven. Bake for 35 to 40 minutes (set your timer).

Test for doneness by rapping the bread with your knuckles; if it sounds hollow, the bread is done; if not, let it bake a little longer and test again. Transfer the bread to a wire rack to cool—top side up—to room temperature before cutting.

Double the ingredients to make 2 loaves.

Main Courses
Fish · Poultry · Meat

STUFFED STRIPED BASS

(SERVES 6)

> 1 striped bass, 3½ to 4 pounds, dressed, head and tail
>   left on
> 1 teaspoon salt
> Freshly ground black pepper
> 1 cup coarsely broken saltine crackers
> ¼ pound raw shrimps, cleaned, shelled, and coarsely
>   chopped
> ¼ cup melted butter
> ¼ cup finely chopped scallions
> 2 tablespoons finely chopped parsley
> ¼ teaspoon crumbled dried thyme
> 2 tablespoons vegetable oil
> 6 lemon wedges

Preheat oven to 400° F.

Wash the fish inside and out under cold running water. Pat it dry inside and out with paper towels. On each side of the fish, spaced evenly apart, make 3 parallel diagonal cuts, each one about 3 inches long and ¼ inch deep. Sprinkle the fish inside and out with the salt and pepper to taste, and set aside.

Put the crackers, shrimps, melted butter, scallions, parsley, and thyme in a mixing bowl; using a wooden spoon, combine them thoroughly. Spoon the mixture into the cavity of the fish, packing it in.

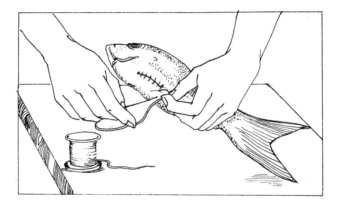

With needle and heavy white thread, sew the opening closed with large overcast stitches, or close it securely with small poultry skewers. If you wish, lace the skewers together with kitchen cord.

Coat the whole fish with the 2 tablespoons vegetable oil, dribbling it on the fish and spreading it with your hands or with a bit of paper towel.

Transfer the fish to a large shallow roasting pan, set it on the middle shelf of the oven, and bake for 35 to 40 minutes (set your timer). Test for doneness by inserting the tips of fork tines into the thickest part of the fish. If the fish comes apart easily and looks opaque, all of the fish is done. If it is not done, bake a little longer and test again.

Remove the pan from the oven. With the aid of 2 pancake

spatulas, lift the fish onto a large heated serving platter. Remove the stitching and surround the fish with lemon wedges.

NOTES:

Red snapper of the same weight may be used in place of striped bass.

In place of the raw shrimps in the filling, ¼ pound fresh crabmeat may be used.

STRIPED BASS ELEANOR

Eleanor Friede (our publisher) has often spoken of "a light, fresh-tasting fish dish" she enjoys very much. Composed of striped bass and Little Neck clams, it's a specialty at one of New York City's finest Italian restaurants. Eleanor confesses to asking, when making a lunch date, if her guest likes fish. If the answer is "yes," off they go to the restaurant, ordering bass on arrival, as it takes 40 minutes to prepare. Brought to the table on its heatproof platter straight from the oven, the bass is then boned and served; perfect for two. Having lunch with Eleanor at the Italian restaurant was the inspiration for this adaptation of the delightful original.

Choose a fresh striped bass weighing about 5 pounds. Have your fish dealer clean and fillet it. Weighed together, the fillets should come to about 2 pounds. A *must* for this dish is Little Neck clams, the smallest variety on the market. Each clam should measure no more than 2 inches around its girth.

(SERVES 4)

2 pounds fillets of striped bass
½ teaspoon salt
1 tablespoon lemon juice
½ teaspoon freshly ground black pepper
¼ teaspoon crumbled dried orégano
2 tablespoons softened butter
2 tablespoons finely chopped shallots (or ¼ teaspoon
     finely chopped garlic and 2 tablespoons finely
     chopped scallion)
¼ cup dry vermouth
¾ cup water
20 Little Neck clams, scrubbed clean under cold
     running water
2 tablespoons chopped fresh parsley

Preheat oven to 350° F.
Wash the fillets well under cold running water. Pat them dry

with paper towels. Skin side down, sprinkle them with the salt, lemon juice, pepper, and orégano.

Cut each fillet into halves, slicing crosswise and at a slight angle, to have 4 pieces equal in size.

With the 2 teaspoons softened butter, grease a shallow 10 × 14 × 2-inch heatproof baking dish that has a tight-fitting cover. Spread the shallots on the bottom of the baking dish, and lay the fish pieces on them. Pour the vermouth and then the water over the fish. Add the clams, hinge side down, arranging some against the inner rim of the dish and the rest between the fillet pieces.

Place the baking dish over high heat and bring the liquid to a boil. Immediately, turn off the heat, cover the dish tightly, and place it on the middle shelf of the oven. Bake for 17 minutes (set your timer).

Test for doneness by inserting the tips of fork tines into the thickest part of one piece of fish. If the fish comes apart easily and looks opaque, all the fish is done. If it is not done, cover and bake for a few minutes longer.

Remove the baking dish from the oven. With a metal spatula transfer the fish to a warm serving platter. (If the clams have not yet opened, first cover the fish with aluminum foil to keep warm on the platter; cover the baking dish tightly, set it over high heat, and steam the clams for 2 or 3 minutes until they open. Discard clams that do not open.) Tilt the clams as you remove them from the baking dish so their juice is added to the sauce, and arrange them around the fish. Add the parsley to the sauce. Immediately, ladle the sauce over the fish and clams. Pour any remaining sauce into a sauceboat and serve it separately (see Note).

NOTE:
If you prefer the fish and clams bathed more generously with this delicate fish broth, serve them in shallow soup plates and provide soup spoons in addition to forks.

HADDOCK MÉDITERRANÉE

The recipe calls for haddock steaks because they're so easily served, but any white-fleshed fish may be used instead. The fish needn't be cut into steaks; large fillets, or even whole fish, work wonderfully. It's the sauce that gives the dish its character—made with tomatoes, garlic, and olive oil as in Provence.

If you substitute other fish for the 1-inch-thick haddock steaks, the baking time may need adjusting, but this presents no problem: test for doneness with the tines of a fork as described in the recipe.

(SERVES 6)

> 6 haddock steaks, cut 1 inch thick
> 3 large tomatoes, skinned, seeded, then coarsely chopped
> 1/4 cup olive oil
> 1 large onion, thinly sliced
> 1 teaspoon finely chopped garlic (1 medium-sized clove)
> 1/4 cup clam juice
> 1/4 cup chicken broth, homemade or canned
> 1/2 cup white wine
> Salt (depending on saltiness of broth)
> Freshly ground black pepper
> 1 teaspoon fennel seeds, crushed with a pestle in a mortar
> 2 tablespoons chopped fresh parsley
> 1 tablespoon freshly grated lemon rind

Preheat oven to 375° F.

Wash the haddock steaks under cold running water, pat them dry with paper towels, and set aside.

Place the tomatoes into boiling water. After 15 to 20 seconds, remove them with a slotted spoon and set them aside until cool enough to handle. Skin them with a small sharp knife, then cut them into quarters. Press each quarter to remove the seeds, chop the tomatoes coarsely, and set them aside.

Place a 10-inch skillet over high heat and pour in the olive oil. When the oil is very hot, stir in the onion slices and let them cook until they are transparent. Stir in the garlic and let it cook for 2 minutes. Add the tomatoes. Turn heat to high; stirring with a wooden spoon from time to time, let the vegetables cook until all the liquid has evaporated. *Remove from heat.*

Transfer the contents of the skillet to an ovenproof dish 10 × 14 inches, or one large enough to hold the haddock steaks in a single layer. Use your wooden spoon to remove all the mixture from the skillet and add it to the dish. Arrange the haddock steaks in one layer on the tomato mixture. Pour the clam juice into the dish, then the broth and the wine. Sprinkle the fish with salt if needed, and with pepper to taste. Scatter the crushed fennel seeds over, then the parsley and grated lemon rind.

Cover the dish with a piece of buttered wax paper, buttered side down, and place it on the middle shelf of the oven. Bake for 12 to 14 minutes (set your timer).

Test for doneness by inserting fork tines into the thickest part of one haddock steak. If the flesh comes apart easily and looks opaque, all the steaks are done. If not, bake for a few minutes longer and test again. Serve the steaks from the ovenproof dish.

BAKED SCALLOPS

(SERVES 8)

> 2 pounds bay or sea scallops
> Salt
> Freshly ground black pepper
> 2 tablespoons fresh lemon juice
> 1/4 cup dry white wine
> 4 tablespoons melted butter
> 1/2 cup heavy cream
> 1/2 cup fresh bread crumbs (see Notes)

Preheat oven to 400° F.

If you use bay scallops, leave them whole; if sea scallops, cut them into quarters. Drain the scallops in a colander. Cover a cookie sheet with 2 layers of paper towels. Spread the scallops out, then pat them dry with more paper towels.

Put the scallops into a large mixing bowl, add the salt and the pepper to taste, then the lemon juice and the white wine. Using your hands, or with a fork and spoon, toss all the ingredients together.

With 2 tablespoons of the melted butter, coat the bottom and sides of a baking dish 12 × 16 inches. Using a rubber spatula, scrape the scallop mixture and all its liquid into the baking dish, then add the cream. Sprinkle top evenly with the bread crumbs, then dribble the remaining 2 tablespoons of melted butter over the crumbs.

Set the baking dish on the middle shelf of the oven and bake for 12 to 14 minutes (set your timer), or until the bread crumbs are pale gold.

NOTES:
As a first course, this dish will serve 14 to 16.
Make bread crumbs in a blender from 2 slices of fresh white bread with crusts removed.

CHICKEN PIE

If made with care, you'll find this Chicken Pie somewhat different. You may even think of it as chicken pie *extraordinaire*—chicken chunks, onions, mushrooms, and carrots are all identifiable in a lightly thickened creamy sauce.

Preparing the sauce is a simple procedure, but it is thickened finally with beaten egg yolks, and this step requires your close attention. Before adding the beaten egg yolks to the hot sauce, use a wire whisk to beat a little of the hot sauce into the beaten yolks first. Add this yolk mixture gradually to the hot sauce in the pan while beating it in with the wire whisk. When the sauce is left to simmer, watch it carefully; if allowed to come to a boil, it will curdle. These directions apply whenever beaten egg yolks are used as a thickening agent for any hot sauce.

(SERVES 6)

CHICKEN
1 roasting chicken, 3½ pounds, quartered
4 cups chicken broth, homemade or canned
2 celery ribs
2 carrots
½ teaspoon peppercorns
1 large bay leaf
1 large onion, sliced
1 parsley sprig

GARNITURES
18 small white onions
½ pound mushrooms, stem bottoms shaved off;
    mushrooms halved
½ teaspoon salt
2 cups cold water
1 teaspoon fresh lemon juice

SAUCE

4 tablespoons butter
4 tablespoons flour
3 egg yolks (U.S. Graded Large)
1 teaspoon fresh lemon juice

PASTRY

½ recipe Pseudo Puff Pastry (p. 39)

GLAZE

1 egg
2 tablespoons cream or milk

Preheat oven to 375° F.

Arrange chicken legs and thighs in a 4- to 6-quart casserole that has a tight-fitting cover, and pour the broth over. Add the celery, carrots, peppercorns, bay leaf, onion slices, and the parsley sprig. Cover the casserole, place it on the middle shelf of the oven, and poach the chicken for 15 minutes (set your timer). Add the chicken breasts, cover the casserole, and poach for 45 minutes more (set your timer).

Test for doneness by inserting the tip of a small sharp knife in the thickest part of a thigh. If the juice runs clear with no trace of pink, all the chicken is done. If it does not, cover the casserole, poach for 5 minutes more, and test again.

Remove the casserole from the oven, and *turn off heat.* Using a slotted spoon, transfer the carrots to a plate and reserve them. With tongs, transfer the chicken pieces to a plate and let them cool. Strain the broth through a fine sieve into a heatproof bowl, pressing down hard on the solids in the sieve to extract their juice. Discard the solids remaining in the sieve. Set the broth aside.

GARNITURES

Put the onions into a medium-sized saucepan with water to cover, and bring to a boil over high heat. Reduce heat to medium, and let the onions simmer for 8 to 10 minutes. Drain, then set the onions aside to cool. When the onions are cool enough to handle, peel them, sprinkle with half of the salt, then set aside.

Put the mushroom halves into a small saucepan and add 2 cups water. Stir in the teaspoon of lemon juice (this prevents discoloration of the mushrooms), and bring the liquid to a boil over high heat. Immediately reduce the heat and let the mushrooms simmer for 4 minutes (set your timer). Drain, then lay the mushrooms out on paper towels. Pat them dry with more paper towels, sprinkle with the remaining salt, and set aside.

When the chicken has cooled, remove and discard the skin. Take the meat off the bones in large pieces, cut it into 2-inch chunks, and set aside.

SAUCE

Melt the butter in a 1½- to 2-quart heavy saucepan over medium heat. When the butter melts, add the flour, blending it in with a wooden spoon until it is smooth. Let the mixture cook until lightly colored, 2 or 3 minutes. Still over heat, gradually add the reserved strained broth, beating it into the mixture with a whisk. Raise the heat to high; continuing to beat, let the mixture come to a boil. Immediately reduce heat to low, and let the sauce simmer for 5 minutes (set your timer).

Meanwhile, beat the egg yolks together in a small bowl. Add a little of the hot sauce to the beaten yolks, beating it in with a whisk, then whisk the yolk mixture into the sauce in the saucepan. Let the sauce cook for about 2 minutes more; do not let it come close to the boil or it will curdle. *Remove the saucepan from heat.* Stir in the teaspoon of lemon juice, taste for salt and pepper, and set aside.

Center an inverted glass ovenproof custard cup in a shallow baking dish, 10 × 14 × 2 inches. (This is a device to keep the pastry top from collapsing into the sauce.) Cover the bottom of the casserole with the chicken chunks, then top them with the reserved carrots, the onions, and the mushrooms. Pour the sauce over the ingredients, and set the dish aside to cool to room temperature.

PASTRY

Remove the pastry from the refrigerator. Dust your work surface lightly with flour. Unwrap the pastry, dust it lightly with flour, and begin to roll it out into a rectangle. Evenly distributing your weight on the handles of the rolling pin, roll it on the pastry all the way to the edges, first away from yourself then back toward yourself. Continue rolling it out until the rectangle measures approximately 12 inches wide, 16 inches long, and $1/8$ inch thick.

Set the baking dish of cooled chicken next to and parallel with the rectangle of pastry. Place the rolling pin on the part of the pastry farthest from you. With the aid of a metal spatula, lift the far edge of the pastry onto the back of the rolling pin. Using your fingertips, lightly press the pastry against the back of the rolling pin—just enough to make it adhere—and roll the pastry toward yourself, *making 1 complete turn.*

Lift the pastry-covered rolling pin by the handles, allowing the remainder of the pastry to hang down freely. Suspending the free pastry just above the baking dish, bring it forward to the edge of the dish nearest you. Let about 1 inch of the pastry drop over the front edge of the dish. Now, unrolling away from yourself, let the pastry fall slackly over the dish and the inverted cup. Keep the rolling pin above the edge of the dish when unrolling; the weight of the rolling pin on the edge or on the cup can cut the pastry.

There will be an overhang of about 1 inch of pastry all around the baking dish. Working with a light touch, and never stretching the pastry, press the edge of the pastry to the outside of the dish and completely enclose the contents. Place the chicken pie in the refrigerator to chill for 20 minutes (set your timer), and *preheat oven to 375° F.*

Remove chicken pie from refrigerator. With a small sharp knife, or with a 1-inch round cookie cutter, cut out 2 circles of pastry to make openings, each about 1 inch in diameter. Center these openings between the cup and the edges of the casserole. This will allow the steam to escape, and keep the pastry from becoming soggy.

Beat the egg and cream (or milk) together; using a pastry brush, paint a film of this mixture over the pastry. With a small sharp knife, score the entire surface of the pastry; make these crisscross slashes no more than $\frac{1}{16}$ inch deep, so as not to cut through the pastry.

Place the pie on the middle shelf of the oven, and bake for 35 minutes (set your timer), or until the pastry is deep golden brown.

NOTES:

If there's filling left over, it may be served on top of Puff Pastry Rounds (p. 37).

If the sauce is too thick, thin it with homemade or canned chicken broth. Remember to keep it from coming to a boil, or the egg yolks will curdle.

Although slightly rich in flavor, Cream Cheese Pastry (p. 24) may be substituted for the Pseudo Puff Pastry.

ROAST CHICKEN BIJOU

Separating the chicken's skin from the meat creates a space into which herb butter is inserted. Spread directly on the meat, the butter makes the chicken self-basting throughout the roasting and flavors it at the same time. The skin, left intact along the full length of the breastbone, inflates and tautens during the roasting. Herb-flecked droplets of butter glisten under the taut skin, giving Roast Chicken Bijou a truly jewellike appearance.

An inexpensive but elegant dish, it can be served hot, at room temperature, or cold, and is an excellent choice for a picnic.

(SERVES 4)

> 1 chicken, 2½ pounds, whole
> 4 tablespoons unsalted butter
> 2 teaspoons crumbled dried tarragon
> 2 tablespoons finely chopped fresh parsley
> Freshly ground black pepper
> ½ teaspoon salt
> Additional salt

Wipe the chicken thoroughly dry inside and out with paper towels. Set it aside.

Place the butter, tarragon, and parsley in a small bowl; using a wooden spoon, cream them together until the ingredients are well blended. Set it aside.

Preheat oven to 375° F.

Slip your finger into the neck opening of the chicken between the skin and the meat beneath; leaving the skin attached only the full length of the breastbone, separate the remaining skin from the meat of the breast, thighs, and drumsticks. When you cannot reach farther down the front of the chicken from the top end, begin again by inserting your finger between skin and meat at the cavity end. Separate skin from meat all around the thighs and drumsticks, but leave the back skin and meat intact.

To spread the creamed herb butter between the skin and the

meat begin again at the neck end. Insert a lump of the herb butter between the skin and the meat. Now, work with your fingers from the outside, pressing the skin so as to move the herb butter. Let the green parsley flecks, visible through the skin, guide you. Because the butter is soft, you can easily manipulate it; spread it over the breast and down toward the thighs. Again, working from the cavity end, spread the herb butter on the meat all around the thighs and drumsticks. Continue until all the herb butter is used.

Dust the cavity of the chicken with the pepper and ½ teaspoon salt.

Using your favorite method, truss the chicken. Place the trussed chicken, breast side up, on a rack set in a roasting pan. Sprinkle the chicken lightly with salt, and place the pan on the lower middle shelf of the oven. Roast for 60 minutes (set your timer).

To test for doneness, remove the pan from the oven. Insert the long handle of a wooden spoon into the cavity of the chicken. Lift the chicken with the handle, tilting it to allow the juices to run into the pan. If the juices run clear with no trace of pink, the chicken is done. If not, return to oven and roast for 5 to 10 minutes more.

Transfer the chicken to a warm serving platter. Cut into quarters to serve, using a sharp knife or poultry shears.

CHICKEN IN WHITE-WINE SAUCE

(SERVES 4 TO 6)

CHICKEN
1 roasting chicken, 3½ to 4 pounds, cut into 8 pieces
1½ cups chicken broth, homemade or canned
1½ cups dry white wine
1 large onion, sliced
1 carrot, cut into chunks
1 bay leaf
¼ teaspoon crumbled dried thyme
½ teaspoon peppercorns
Pinch of grated nutmeg

SAUCE
3 tablespoons unsalted butter
4 tablespoons flour
Salt
¼ teaspoon ground white pepper
1 carrot, grated
2 egg yolks (U.S. Graded Large)
¼ cup heavy cream
1 teaspoon fresh lemon juice
2 tablespoons chopped fresh parsley

Preheat oven to 375° F.

Arrange the thighs and drumsticks in a 4- to 6-quart casserole that has a tight-fitting cover. Pour the broth over, then the wine. Add the onion slices, carrot pieces, bay leaf, thyme, peppercorns, and nutmeg. Cover the casserole, place it on the lower middle shelf of the oven, and braise for 15 minutes (set your timer).

Add the chicken breasts, cover the casserole, and braise for 45 minutes more (set your timer), or until the chicken is tender. Test for doneness by removing a thigh with tongs, then inserting the tip of a small sharp knife into its thickest part. If the juice runs clear with no trace of pink, all the chicken is done. If it does not, return the thigh to the casserole, cover, and braise for 5 minutes more, then test again.

Remove the casserole from the oven. Using tongs, transfer the chicken pieces to a heated platter, arranging them attractively. Cover the chicken loosely with aluminum foil to keep it warm.

SAUCE

Set a fine sieve over a large heatproof bowl. Pour the contents of the casserole into the sieve, pressing down on the solids with a wooden spoon to extract all their juice. Discard the solids remaining in the sieve. Return the liquid to the casserole, bring it to a boil over high heat, and let it continue to boil until it is reduced to 2 cups. *Turn off the heat.*

Melt the butter in a 1- or 2-quart heavy saucepan over medium heat. When the butter melts, add the flour, blending it in with a wooden spoon until it is smooth. Let the mixture cook for 2 or 3 minutes. Still over heat, gradually add the reduced liquid, beating it into the flour-butter mixture with a whisk. Raise the heat to high, and let the sauce come to a boil. Immediately, reduce the heat to low. Add salt and pepper to taste. Stir in the grated carrot, and let the sauce simmer for 5 minutes (set your timer).

Meanwhile, beat the egg yolks and heavy cream together. Add a little of the hot sauce to the yolk-cream mixture, beating it in with a whisk. When the timer bell rings, whisk this mixture into the sauce and let it cook for 2 or 3 minutes; watch that it does not come close to a boil or it will curdle. *Remove from the heat.*

Stir in the lemon juice, and add the chopped parsley. Pour half the sauce over the chicken, and serve the rest in a heated sauceboat.

CHICKEN BRAISED IN RED WINE

This chicken dish is an adaptation of the famous French *coq au vin*. Prepared up to the point where the browned chicken in its sauce is assembled in the casserole, it may be refrigerated for up to 24 hours before baking. Transfer it directly from the refrigerator to the preheated oven. *Fleurons*, always made ahead in any case, may be served at room temperature.

(SERVES 6)

GARNITURES
18 small white onions
½ pound salt pork, cut into ½-inch pieces
2 tablespoons butter
½ pound mushrooms, stem bottoms shaved off;
    mushrooms halved

CHICKEN
1 roasting chicken, 3½ to 4 pounds, cut into 12
    approximately equal pieces
Salt
Freshly ground black pepper
Vegetable oil
2 tablespoons chopped fresh parsley

SAUCE
3 tablespoons butter
¼ cup chopped shallots
1 teaspoon chopped garlic (1 medium-sized clove)
4 tablespoons flour
½ cup dry red wine
1½ cups chicken broth, homemade or canned
½ teaspoon crumbled dried thyme
1 large bay leaf

PASTRY
Fleurons (p. 36), *optional*

Put the onions into a medium-sized saucepan with water to cover, and bring to a boil over high heat. Reduce heat to medium, and let the onions simmer for 8 to 10 minutes. Drain, then set the onions aside until they are cool enough to peel.

While the onions cool, prepare the salt pork. Put the salt-pork pieces in a small saucepan with water to cover, and bring the liquid to a boil over high heat. Reduce heat to medium, and let them simmer for 5 minutes (set your timer). Drain the pieces in a fine strainer, then spread them out on paper towels. Pat them dry with more paper towels.

Melt 2 tablespoons butter in a large skillet (10 to 12 inches) over medium heat. Add the salt-pork pieces, stirring them slowly with a wooden spoon and turning them about until they are brown and crisp. Remove the skillet from heat; using a slotted spoon, transfer the browned pieces from the fat to a large bowl.

Peel the cooled onions. Return the skillet of fat to medium heat. When the fat is hot, add the onions; again using the wooden spoon, slowly turn onions about in the fat until they are lightly browned on all sides. With a slotted spoon, transfer onions from the fat to the bowl of browned salt-pork pieces.

Return the skillet of fat to medium heat. When the fat is hot, add the mushroom halves, stirring them with the wooden spoon until lightly colored. Again using the slotted spoon, transfer them from the fat to the other ingredients in the bowl. Set the skillet of fat aside.

CHICKEN

Preheat oven to 375° F.

Lightly sprinkle the chicken pieces with salt and pepper on both sides. Add enough vegetable oil to the fat in the skillet to come up the sides about ⅛ inch. Set the skillet over medium heat. When the oil is very hot, add the chicken pieces and brown them on both sides, using tongs to turn them. As the pieces brown, use tongs to transfer them from the pan to a large, heavy baking dish, 10 × 14 × 2 inches. Set the baking dish of browned chicken aside. Pour off all the fat from the skillet, leaving the brown bits clinging to the bottom and sides, and prepare the sauce.

SAUCE

Add 3 tablespoons butter to the skillet over low heat. When the butter melts, add the shallots and garlic, stirring them into the butter with a wooden spoon and scraping in all the brown bits adhering to the bottom and sides of the skillet. Let the mixture cook for 2 or 3 minutes.

Add the flour, blending it in with a wooden spoon, and let the mixture cook until it is smooth and lightly colored, another 2 or 3 minutes. Stirring constantly, gradually add the wine and, still stirring, the chicken broth, thyme, and bay leaf. Turn the heat to high and bring the liquid to a boil. Immediately reduce the heat and let the sauce simmer for 5 minutes (set your timer). Taste for salt and pepper, and *remove the skillet from the heat.*

Top the chicken in the baking dish with the salt-pork pieces, onions, and mushrooms. Using a fine sieve, strain the sauce over the chicken, pressing down on the solids in the sieve to extract their juice. Discard the solids remaining in the sieve. Cover the dish tightly with aluminum foil, place it on the middle shelf of the oven, and braise for 30 minutes (set your timer).

Test for doneness by removing a thigh, then inserting the tip of a small sharp knife into its thickest part. If it pierces easily, all the chicken is done. If it is resistant, return it to the dish, cover the dish tightly with the aluminum foil, braise for 5 minutes more, then test again.

Remove the dish from the oven. Sprinkle the chicken with the chopped parsley. If you serve it with *fleurons,* arrange them attractively around the inner rim of the baking dish.

STUFFED CHICKEN DRUMSTICKS

Served hot or at room temperature, these are elegant to look at and definitely a taste surprise. Lovers of chicken breast may well be lured away by these delicious drumsticks.

(SERVES 4 TO 6)

> ## STUFFING
> ¼ pound butter (1 stick)
> 3½ cups fresh bread crumbs (See Notes.)
> ½ cup chopped scallions
> ¼ cup chopped fresh parsley
> 1 teaspoon salt
> ¼ teaspoon freshly ground black pepper
> ½ teaspoon dried thyme

Melt ¼ pound butter in a large heavy skillet over medium heat. Add the bread crumbs; with a wooden spoon, stir them constantly as they toast, darkening evenly, to pale nut-brown. This will take about 10 minutes.

When the bread crumbs are toasted, spoon them into a medium-sized bowl, where they will continue to darken slightly on their own. Add the scallions, parsley, salt, pepper to taste, and thyme. Lightly toss the ingredients together, and set aside.

Preheat oven to 350° F.

> ## DRUMSTICKS
> 12 chicken drumsticks, about 4 ounces each
> 4 teaspoons softened butter
> Melted butter
> Salt
> Pepper

Have at hand 12 small metal skewers—the most effective little tools for keeping the stuffing in.

In one hand, hold the drumstick, broad meaty end up, with narrow tip end set firmly on the work surface. With a small sharp

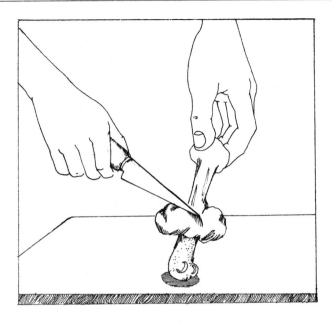

knife in the other hand, insert the tip of the knife between the
meat and the bone that is exposed at the top of the broad end.
Begin to scrape the meat from the bone. Scrape it away and down-
ward toward the tip end; at the same time turn the drumstick
slowly, twirling it as you would an umbrella on its tip.

Let the meat fall freely over the tip end. If you come to a
tendon as you scrape, give it a knick with your knife and cut it off.

When all the meat is scraped away from the bone and overhangs
the tip end, place the drumstick on the work surface so that it lies
horizontally. Using a sharp cleaver, chop the bone off with one
blow.

Prepare the remaining drumsticks.

One at a time, reconstruct each drumstick: bring up the meat
and skin, hold it together loosely, and spoon some of the stuffing
into the cavity. Pack it down to the bottom with your finger.
Continue filling and packing the cavity just short of the top. Fold
the skin flap over, and skewer it to the meat. Repeat with remaining drumsticks, and set aside.

With the 4 teaspoons of softened butter, coat the whole inside of a baking dish large enough to hold the drumsticks in one layer with some space between them. Arrange the drumsticks in it, brush the tops with melted butter, and season with salt and pepper. Place on the middle shelf of the oven and bake for 45 minutes, basting every 10 minutes or so with the butter in the baking dish.

NOTES:
The drumstick bones, rich in marrow, add flavor when used in making chicken stock.

All ingredients may be doubled to make 24 drumsticks. Be sure to bake in a pan large enough to hold them in one layer so they will brown evenly. If a large pan is unavailable, make in small batches.

There's little chance of having leftovers, but if you have some, refrigerate them. Cut into thinly sliced rounds, and brought to room temperature, they are delightful accompaniments with drinks.

Make bread crumbs in a blender from 7 slices of white bread with crusts removed.

ROAST DUCKS WITH CRANBERRY SAUCE

An invitation to lecture and work with the students at Cornell University's prestigious Hotel School inspired the recipe for this dish. Devised in Shoreham, Long Island, it was entitled Ducks Shoreham, and is probably listed that way in the school's records. Renamed, the dish is described more accurately, but still gives no hint of its outstanding feature—its crispness.

A few simple devices insure crispness. First, as much moisture as possible must be removed from the ducks. Stuffing them with paper towels does the trick. By the time the sauce is made, the paper has absorbed the moisture. Placing the ducks on the rack apart from each other, so they will not touch while roasting, prevents soft, unbrowned spots. Fat dripping into the pan has a certain amount of moisture from the ducks and must be poured off; otherwise the birds will steam rather than roast. Uniform, allover browning is achieved by turning the ducks as described in the recipe. The best time to turn them is when pouring off the fat. Follow the suggested instructions for pouring off the fat. You'll find this the most convenient way to dispose of it.

Fruit usually accompanies duck, but not for decorative reasons; acid in fruit cuts fattiness. There will be very little, if any, residual fat in these birds, but the skin and meat will be rich. As if made for each other, the tartness of cranberries—high in acid—complements perfectly the rich flavor of duck.

(SERVES 8)

> ### DUCKS
> 2 ducks, 5 to 6 pounds each, eviscerated, necks and
>   gizzards reserved
> 1 teaspoon salt
> ½ teaspoon freshly ground black pepper
> 1 large onion
> 2 large garlic cloves

SAUCE

2 tablespoons butter
1 cup chopped onion (1 large onion)
¼ cup diced carrot
¼ cup diced celery
½ teaspoon crumbled dried thyme
1½ cups dry red wine
2 cups chicken broth, homemade or canned
2 parsley sprigs
½ cup whole cranberries
¼ to ½ cup red-currant jelly
¼ cup Crème de Cassis liqueur
2 tablespoons arrowroot
1 tablespoon water

Pat the ducks dry inside and out with paper towels. With a small sharp knife, cut off the second section of each wing by severing it at the joint. Reserve these wing sections. Cut away and discard all visible fat from the neck and cavity ends of each duck. Stuff the ducks tightly with paper towels, then wrap them in several layers of paper towels. Set the ducks aside.

SAUCE

With a cleaver, chop the reserved necks and wing sections into ½-inch pieces. Slice the reserved gizzards into ¼-inch pieces. Melt the butter in a 10-inch skillet over medium heat. When the butter is hot, add these pieces; stirring from time to time with a wooden spoon, brown them evenly on all sides.

Stir in the chopped onion, carrot, and celery, and let them cook until the onion is light brown. Add the crumbled thyme, then pour in the wine. Stir the ingredients together, then let the mixture cook for 5 minutes (set your timer). Pour in the chicken broth, raise the heat to high, add the parsley sprigs, and bring the liquid to a boil. Immediately, reduce the heat, partially cover the skillet, and let the sauce simmer for 1½ hours (set your timer).

While the sauce simmers, wash the cranberries under cold running water, and remove any stems. Put the washed berries in a small saucepan, add water to cover, set the pan over high heat, and bring the liquid to a boil. Reduce the heat, and let the berries simmer until their skins "pop"; this will take only a minute or two. *Remove from heat.*

Drain the berries immediately, then spread them out on paper towels. Pat them dry with more paper towels. Transfer the berries to a cutting board and, using a sharp knife, chop them coarsely. Set them aside.

Preheat oven to 450° F.

When the timer bell rings, remove the skillet of sauce from the heat. Strain the sauce through a fine sieve into a heatproof bowl, pressing down on the solids with a wooden spoon to extract their juice. Discard the solids remaining in the sieve.

Return the strained sauce to the skillet. Stir in $\frac{1}{4}$ cup of the currant jelly and let it melt in the sauce over low heat. Add the chopped berries, then the Crème de Cassis, stirring these ingredients through. Taste for salt and pepper. Also, if sauce is too tart for your taste, melt into the sauce as much of the remaining currant jelly as you wish. Remove the skillet from the heat, and set the sauce aside.

DUCKS

Unwrap the ducks, and remove the paper towels from the cavities. Season the cavities with the salt and pepper. Cut the large onion into halves, then crush the garlic cloves with the broad side of a knife. Put $\frac{1}{2}$ onion and 1 crushed garlic clove into each cavity. Using your favorite method, truss the ducks.

Sprinkle the trussed ducks lightly with salt. Set a rack in a shallow roasting pan, arrange the ducks, breast side up, on the rack, far apart enough so they do not touch each other. Place the pan on the middle shelf of the oven, and roast for 30 minutes (set your timer).

While the ducks roast, prepare counter space close to the oven with a good thickness of newspaper, and set on it a large empty coffee can or some other large heatproof disposable container. When the timer bell rings, remove the pan from the oven. Set the rack of ducks aside, and pour off the fat from the pan into the disposable container. Return the rack to the pan. Using a kitchen towel, turn the ducks over so they are breast side down and not touching each other. Return to the middle shelf of the oven and roast for another 30 minutes (set your timer).

When the timer bell rings, again remove the pan from the oven and pour off all fat from the pan into the disposable container. Turn the ducks over so they are breast side up and not touching each other. Return to the middle shelf of the oven to roast for the last 30 minutes (set your timer). If you prefer duck especially well done, let them roast for another 15 minutes.

Remove the pan from the oven. Transfer the ducks to a heated serving platter, remove the trussing cords, and cover the ducks loosely with aluminum foil to keep them warm.

Pour off all the fat from the pan into the disposable container. Add the sauce to the pan and place it over medium heat. With a metal spatula, scrape in any brown bits adhering to the bottom and sides of the pan, and bring the sauce to a simmer. Combine 2 tablespoons arrowroot with 1 tablespoon water, then stir it into the sauce. Let the sauce simmer until it thickens, about 6 minutes.

To serve, carve the ducks or quarter them with poultry shears. Serve the sauce in a *heated* sauceboat.

PHEASANT WITH SOUR-CREAM SAUCE

Because sour cream curdles if brought to a boil, almost all recipes instruct you to add it to a hot sauce at the last moment and simply heat it through. When served in this fashion, the sauce can therefore be warm only, never hot.

There is, however, a foolproof technique used by Hungarian cooks which prevents sour cream from curdling when brought to a boil. In the proportion of 1 tablespoon flour to 1 cup sour cream, the flour is beaten into the cream; then this mixture is beaten into the hot sauce as it is brought to a boil over high heat. The sauce is then allowed to simmer to the desired consistency.

Perfect with pheasant, sour-cream sauce is subtly tart, velvety in texture, and—thanks to Hungarian cooks—comes to the table hot. We must be grateful to them; the method works with any other hot sauce requiring the addition of sour cream.

(SERVES 6)

> 2 oven-ready pheasants, 3 to 3½ pounds each, necks and gizzards reserved
> ½ teaspoon salt combined with a little freshly ground black pepper
> 4 tablespoons unsalted butter
> 2 tablespoons vegetable oil
> ½ cup finely chopped shallots
> ¼ cup Cognac
> 1 cup dry white wine
> 1 cup chicken broth, homemade or canned
> 1 cup sour cream
> 1 tablespoon flour
> 1 tablespoon tomato paste

Preheat oven to 350° F.

Pat the pheasants dry inside and out with paper towels. Sprinkle the cavity of each with half of the combined salt and pepper. Using your favorite method, truss the pheasants and then set them aside.

Chop the reserved necks and gizzards into approximately ¼-inch pieces, and set them aside.

Over medium heat, melt the butter and oil in a 4- to 6-quart heavy casserole that has a tight-fitting cover. When the butter and oil are very hot, add the pheasants; still on medium heat, brown them. Clasp birds firmly between 2 wooden spoons and turn each one from time to time until the birds are browned on all sides.

Transfer the pheasants to a plate, and set them aside.

Stir the chopped necks and gizzards into the hot fat and let them cook until lightly brown. Reduce the heat, add the shallots, and let them cook for 1 minute. Return the pheasants to the casserole, pouring in any juices accumulated on the plate. Immediately warm the Cognac in a small saucepan over low heat. Turn off the heat and, standing back, ignite the Cognac. Pour it flaming over the pheasants in the casserole. When the flame dies out, add the white wine to the casserole, then the chicken broth. Raise the heat to high, and bring the liquids to a boil. *Immediately turn off heat.*

Cover the casserole tightly, place it on the middle shelf of the oven, and braise for 30 minutes (set your timer). Test for doneness by inserting the tip of a small sharp knife into the thickest part of a thigh. If the juice runs clear with no trace of pink, the pheasants are done. If it does not, cover, braise for 5 minutes more (set your timer), and test again.

Transfer the pheasants to a heated platter, remove the trussing cords, and cover the pheasants loosely with aluminum foil to keep them warm.

Set the casserole over high heat and bring the liquid to a boil. Let it continue to boil until it has reduced to 1½ cups. Strain the liquid through a sieve into a medium-sized heatproof bowl, pressing down on the solids with a wooden spoon to extract all their juice. Discard the solids remaining in the sieve. Return the liquid to the casserole and set it over low heat.

Beating with a small wire whisk, thoroughly combine the sour cream with the flour and tomato paste. Still beating, whisk this mixture into the liquid in the casserole. Raise the heat to high and, continuing to whisk, bring the liquid to a boil. Immediately reduce heat, and let the sauce simmer for 5 minutes (set your timer). Taste for salt and pepper, and *remove from heat.*

Serve the pheasants, cut lengthwise into halves with poultry shears, on a heated platter. Serve the sauce in a *heated* sauceboat.

ROAST FILET OF BEEF ON PUFF PASTRY ROUNDS

As chefs would say, a filet of beef and puff pastry should "marry well." They do, but not when the filet is enclosed by the pastry and they bake together. Wrapped in the pastry, the beef steams rather than roasts; the puff pastry, meant to rise in paper-thin layers, doesn't really rise and turns soggy. Preparing the filet of beef and puff pastry as described in this recipe, the best qualities of both are preserved since each keeps its characteristic flavor and texture.

Served along with Sauce Madeira, tender slices of roast filet of beef overlapped on flaky puff-pastry rounds make a superb combination.

(SERVES 6)

SAUCE
2 tablespoons butter
¼ cup chopped shallots
½ pound mushrooms, finely chopped
1½ cups homemade beef broth, or homemade or canned chicken broth
1 tablespoon tomato paste
1 tablespoon meat glaze
¼ teaspoon crumbled dried thyme
¼ cup Madeira
2 teaspoons arrowroot mixed with 1 tablespoon water

FILET
3 pounds center-cut filet of beef, trimmed of all fat, tied in 4 places
2 tablespoons softened butter
1½ teaspoons salt
½ teaspoon freshly ground black pepper

PASTRY
6 baked Puff Pastry Rounds (p. 37), arranged on a cookie sheet, and set aside

Over medium heat, melt the butter in an 8- to 10-inch skillet that has a tight-fitting cover. Stir in the shallots and let them cook until they are transparent. Add the mushrooms, reduce the heat to low, cover the skillet, and let them cook until soft, 4 to 6 minutes.

Remove the cover, turn the heat to medium-high, and cook until the liquid has evaporated. Immediately pour in the home-made beef broth or chicken broth, dissolve the tomato paste in it, then the meat glaze, and add the thyme. Raise the heat and bring the liquid to a boil. Reduce the heat, and let the sauce simmer, uncovered, for 20 minutes (set your timer). Turn off heat, and let the sauce stand uncovered. Keep the Madeira and arrowroot mixture nearby for finishing the sauce later.

FILET

Preheat oven to 450° F.

Spread the entire surface of the meat with the softened butter, then sprinkle it with the salt and pepper. Center the filet on a rack set in a large shallow roasting pan, place it on the middle shelf of the oven, and roast for 30 minutes (set your timer).

Turn off heat. Remove the pan from oven, and place the cookie sheet of Puff Pastry Rounds on the middle shelf to warm.

Transfer the roast to a heated serving platter, cut and remove the trussing cord, and cover the roast loosely with aluminum foil to keep it warm.

Finishing the sauce

Pour off and discard any fat accumulated in the roasting pan. Add the reserved sauce to the roasting pan. Use a rubber spatula to get all of the sauce into the pan. Set the pan over medium heat; using a metal spatula, scrape in any brown bits adhering to the bottom and sides of the pan. Pour in the Madeira, stir the arrow-root-water mixture to redissolve it, and add it to the pan. Reduce the heat and let the sauce simmer until it thickens slightly, 6 to 8 minutes. Taste for salt and pepper, then pour the sauce into a heated sauceboat.

To serve

Present the filet carved into ¾-inch-thick slices, the warmed Puff Pastry Rounds arranged along the farther edge of the platter which is free of meat juices. When serving, put a pastry round on each dinner plate, then overlap 2 or 3 slices of filet on top of the round. Serve the sauce from the sauceboat.

NOTES:
If you must use canned broth, use canned chicken broth because it is more neutral in flavor; canned beef broth is usually overpowering for this type of dish.

FLEMISH BEEF STEW

(SERVES 6)

> 3 pounds ½-inch boneless chuck, cut into pieces 2 × 3½ inches, all excess fat removed
> ½ pound lean slab bacon in 1 piece
> 1 teaspoon salt
> ½ teaspoon freshly ground black pepper
> 6 cups thinly sliced onions (approximately 6 large onions)
> 1 teaspoon finely chopped garlic (1 medium-sized clove)
> ½ cup flour
> 1½ cups dark beer
> 2 cups homemade beef broth, or homemade or canned chicken broth
> 1 large bay leaf
> ½ teaspoon crumbled dried thyme
> 2 teaspoons sugar
> 3 tablespoons wine vinegar
> 2 tablespoons chopped fresh parsley

Pat the beef pieces dry with paper towels and set them aside.

Cut the bacon across the grain into ¼-inch slices, and lay them out in a 10- to 12-inch skillet. Cook the bacon over low heat until the fat begins to melt, then turn the heat to medium and let bacon cook until crisp. Watch that it does not burn. Using a slotted spoon, remove the cooked bacon, and let it drain on paper towels. Set the skillet of fat aside.

Preheat oven to 375° F.

Sprinkle each piece of meat with salt and pepper. Set the skillet of fat over medium heat. When the fat is very hot, add the meat pieces; using tongs to turn them over, brown the pieces on both sides. Brown them in batches; as they brown, transfer them with the tongs to a shallow ovenproof casserole 10 × 14 × 2 inches.

Set the browned meat aside, then add to the skillet, still over medium heat, all the sliced onions. Use a metal spatula to turn them every few minutes so that they brown evenly. When all the onions are evenly brown, add the garlic, stir it through, and cook for 2 or 3 minutes more.

Add the flour, stirring it in with a wooden spoon to blend it well with the onions and garlic, then let the mixture cook for 2 or 3 minutes. Still over heat and stirring constantly, gradually add the beer, then the broth. Add the bay leaf, thyme, and sugar. Stir them through, raise the heat to high, and bring the mixture to a boil. Immediately, reduce the heat and let the sauce simmer for 5 minutes (set your timer).

Pour the sauce over the meat, cover the casserole tightly with aluminum foil, place it on the lower middle shelf of the oven, and braise the meat for 1½ hours (set your timer).

Test for doneness by inserting the tip of a sharp knife into one piece of meat. If it pierces easily, all the meat is done. If it is resistant, cover the casserole, braise for 5 minutes more, and test again.

Remove the casserole from the oven. Stir in the vinegar, then sprinkle the top of the meat with the parsley and the bacon.

NOTES:

If you're fortunate enough to have venison, by all means use it in place of the boneless chuck.

Because of the robust flavor of this dish, it is better to use chicken rather than beef broth if you must use canned broth. Canned chicken broth is more neutral in flavor; the flavor of canned beef broth overpowers the natural flavor of the stew. Homemade beef broth is ideal, of course, but success with the dish does not depend on it.

SAUERBRATEN

In its native Germany, *Sauerbraten* varies from region to region and even from household to household. Small shifts in procedure, or a few special ingredients passed down as family secrets, make each version different from any other. But a successful *Sauerbraten* gains its unique flavor primarily from the long marinating process. If you have a sudden craving for the dish, it can't be made on the spur of the moment. To absorb flavor, the meat in its marinade should remain in the refrigerator for 3 days. It takes that long because refrigeration retards the process. However, if you can set it in a cool room or in a cool basement, reduce the time to 2 days.

This *Sauerbraten* will also be different from others you've tasted because of a "family secret" which helps to improve the dish: the meat gains in flavor when it is in sliced form during the last 30 minutes of braising, and it cooks more evenly. And the end pieces will not overcook as they so often do when the meat is not sliced, thus preventing "shredding" when slicing.

(SERVES 6 TO 8)

4 pounds bottom round of beef in 1 piece
2 cups red-wine vinegar
2 cups water
1 large onion, thinly sliced
4 tablespoons vegetable oil or lard
½ cup sliced carrot
1 cup chopped onion (1 large onion)
½ teaspoon finely chopped garlic
1 teaspoon salt
1 cup water
2 bay leaves
3 cloves
½ teaspoon black peppercorns
6 whole juniper berries
¾ cup gingersnap crumbs

Put the piece of bottom round into a large bowl. Pour the vinegar over it, then the 2 cups water, and add the onion slices. Cover the bowl with plastic wrap, and keep it in the refrigerator for 3 days, turning the meat over in the marinade 2 or 3 times a day.

When the meat has marinated for 3 days, remove it from the refrigerator. Take it out of the marinade, and pat it dry with paper towels. Strain the marinade into a bowl, and set it aside. Discard the solids remaining in the strainer.

Preheat oven to 350° F.

Over medium heat, heat the oil or lard in a 4- to 6-quart casserole that has a tight-fitting cover. When the oil is very hot, place the meat in it, fat side down, and brown it. Then, using 2 wooden spoons to turn meat, brown each side completely. Finally, the whole piece of meat should be an evenly colored deep brown. Transfer the meat to a plate, and set it aside.

Pour off and discard all but 3 tablespoons of the fat in the casserole. Return the casserole to medium heat, and stir in the carrot, chopped onion, and garlic. Stirring from time to time, let the vegetables cook until the onion is lightly colored.

Set the meat on the vegetables. Add 3 cups of the marinade to the casserole, stir in the salt, and add the 1 cup water. Add the bay leaves, cloves, black peppercorns, and juniper berries. Raise the heat to high and bring the liquid to a boil. *Turn off heat.* Cover the casserole tightly, place it on the lower middle shelf of the oven, and braise for 1½ hours (set your timer).

Remove the casserole from the oven and transfer the meat to a cutting board. Set a sieve over a medium-sized heatproof bowl. Pour the contents of the casserole into the sieve, pressing down on the solids with a wooden spoon to extract their juice. Discard the solids remaining in the sieve.

Measure off 4 cups of the strained liquid and pour it into the casserole. Stir in ½ cup of the gingersnap crumbs, cover the casserole, and return it to the lower middle shelf of the oven.

Cut the meat into ⅓-inch-thick slices. Check the sauce in the casserole; the gingersnap crumbs will have dissolved. If the sauce seems too thin, add the remaining gingersnap crumbs, then stir to blend them in. Arrange the meat slices in the sauce, cover the casserole tightly, and braise the *Sauerbraten* for 30 minutes more (set your timer). If you wish, serve it directly from the casserole.

BRAISED FRESH BRISKET OF BEEF

(SERVES 4 TO 6)

2½ to 3 pounds fresh brisket of beef (first cut)
1 teaspoon freshly ground black pepper
2 tablespoons vegetable oil
1 medium-sized onion, coarsely chopped
1 celery rib, coarsely chopped
1 medium-sized carrot, coarsely chopped
1 garlic clove, crushed
1 bay leaf
½ cup red wine
2 cups water
½ teaspoon salt
1 parsley sprig

Preheat oven to 375° F.

Pat the meat dry with paper towels. Scatter half of the pepper over one side of the meat and press it in with your hands. Turn the meat over, and press in the remaining pepper. Set the meat aside.

Measure the vegetable oil into a 10- to 12-inch heavy skillet over high heat. When the oil is very hot, add the meat. Brown it well, about 5 minutes on each side. Still over high heat, add the onion, celery, carrot, and garlic to the skillet, stirring them into the oil with a wooden spoon. Shake the pan from time to time to keep the meat from sticking. Stir the vegetables occasionally, turning them over in the oil, and cook until the onion takes on a light brown color.

Add the bay leaf. Pour the wine over the meat and vegetables, then add the water to the skillet. Immediately stir in the salt and add the sprig of parsley. Let the liquid come to the boil, *but watch it*—it will happen quickly. Immediately turn off heat. Cover the skillet tightly with aluminum foil and place it on the lower middle shelf of the oven. Braise the brisket for 2 hours.

Test for doneness by piercing the thickest part of the meat with the tip of a sharp knife. If the meat is resistant, cover and bake for 15 minutes more.

Remove skillet from the oven. Transfer the meat to a carving board or a warm platter, and cover it with aluminum foil to keep it warm.

Set a strainer over a small saucepan. Pour the contents of the skillet into the strainer; with a wooden spoon, press down hard on the vegetables to extract all their juices before discarding them. Keep the saucepan of strained juices warm over medium heat. Carve the meat across the grain into thin slices. Serve the juice separately in a heated sauceboat.

NOTES:
To reheat leftover brisket: Remove from refrigerator; preheat oven to 300° F. Place casserole (with meat in its broth) on the middle shelf of the oven; cover, and heat for 45 minutes.
For other ways to use leftover brisket see Notes following Beef Broth (p. 83).

BRAISED TONGUE

Braised tongue is an excellent main dish to make ahead of time. The tongue in its sauce keeps perfectly in the refrigerator for 3 or 4 days. To reheat, see Notes.

(SERVES 6)

3½ to 4 pounds smoked tongue
1½ cups dry red wine
1½ cups cold water
1 large onion, quartered
1 ripe tomato, quartered
1 carrot
3 cloves
6 peppercorns
1 large bay leaf
4 teaspoons softened butter
4 teaspoons flour
Salt
Pepper

Preheat oven to 350° F.

Put the tongue into a 4- to 6-quart casserole that has a tight-fitting cover. Pour the red wine over, then the water. Add the vegetables, cloves, peppercorns, and bay leaf. Cover the casserole, place it on the middle shelf of the oven, and braise for 1½ hours, or until the tongue is tender. Test for doneness by inserting the tip of a small sharp knife into the root end. If it slides in easily, the tongue is done. If there is resistance, braise for 15 minutes more (set your timer), and test again.

Remove the casserole from the oven and *turn off heat.* Transfer the tongue from the casserole to a platter, and set it aside until it is cool enough to handle. While the tongue cools, prepare the sauce.

Set the casserole over medium heat. With a wooden spoon beat softened butter and flour together to a smooth paste. When the liquid is hot, add the butter-flour paste, beating it in with a wire whisk. Let the sauce cook for 3 or 4 minutes, or until it thickens lightly. Remove from the heat.

Set a fine sieve over a large heatproof bowl. Pour the contents of the casserole into the sieve. With a wooden spoon, press down on the solids in the sieve to extract their juice. Discard the solids remaining in the sieve. Taste the sauce for salt and pepper, and set it aside.

When the tongue is cool enough to handle, skin it with a small sharp knife. Put the skinned tongue into the casserole, and pour the sauce over it. The casserole of tongue in its sauce may be set aside at room temperature for as long as 4 hours before reheating it.

About 30 minutes before you plan to serve the tongue, *preheat oven to 350° F.* Place the casserole on the lower middle shelf of the oven, and reheat the tongue in its sauce for 15 to 20 minutes (set your timer).

Transfer the tongue to a heated platter. Starting at the tip, cut it diagonally into thin slices. Serve the sauce in a heated sauceboat.

NOTES:
To reheat refrigerated casserole of tongue in its sauce, preheat oven to 350° F.
  Cover the casserole, and place it on the middle shelf of the oven for 40
  minutes; this will heat it through.

BRAISED VEAL CHOPS

(SERVES 6)

> 6 veal chops, ¾ inch thick, approximately 2½ to 3
>   pounds
> Salt
> Freshly ground black pepper
> ½ cup flour
> 3 tablespoons butter
> 1 tablespoon vegetable oil
> ¼ cup finely chopped carrot
> ½ cup finely chopped onion
> ½ teaspoon crumbled dried thyme
> ¼ cup dry vermouth
> ½ cup chicken broth, homemade or canned
> 2 tablespoons finely chopped fresh parsley

Preheat oven to 350° F.

Sprinkle the chops lightly with salt and then with pepper, pressing the pepper into the meat. Melt the butter in the oil in a 12-inch skillet over medium heat. Meanwhile, quickly dredge each chop with flour and shake off any excess. When the butter and oil are very hot, add the chops, arranging them so that they fit in one layer. Still over medium heat, let them cook until golden brown on both sides; use tongs to turn them over. Transfer the chops to a plate, and set aside.

Using a wooden spoon, stir the carrot and onion into the hot fat, and cook the vegetables until the onion browns slightly. Scatter the thyme over the vegetables, then pour the vermouth over, and let the mixture come to a boil, *but watch it*—it will happen quickly. Immediately turn off the heat. Transfer all the contents from the skillet to a heatproof dish. Make a bed of the vegetables and place the chops on it, each one slightly overlapping. Add any meat juices that have accumulated on the plate. Cover the dish tightly with aluminum foil and place it on the lower shelf of the oven. Braise the chops for 30 minutes (set your timer).

Test for doneness by using the tip of a sharp knife to make a slit in the fleshiest part of one chop. If the juice runs clear with no trace of pink, the chops are done. If not, cover, braise for 10 minutes more, and test again.

Remove the dish from the oven to the top of the stove. With tongs transfer the chops to a warm platter, arranging them in a row down the center, each one slightly overlapping. Cover them with aluminum foil to keep warm. Add the broth to the vegetables in the dish and bring it to a boil over high heat. Stir in the chopped parsley and turn off the heat. Spoon some of the sauce over each chop and serve the rest in a heated sauceboat.

STUFFED BREAST OF VEAL

Have your butcher bone the breast of veal and make a pocket in it. Be sure to ask for the bones because you will be using them as a rack on which to braise the meat.

The bones, while serving as a rack to keep the meat free of the bottom of the pan, contribute at the same time a most distinctive flavor to the sauce. Breast of veal has little meat and many bones; stuffing this cut of meat makes it go a long way. But the incomparable flavor characteristic of veal bones makes the dish the success it is. It's delicious served hot or at room temperature. Try it sometime as a whole roast for picnic dining; it slices easily.

(SERVES 6 TO 8)

> 4½ to 5 pounds of breast of veal (weight before boning)
> ½ pound lean pork, ground
> ½ pound lean beef, ground
> 1 package (10 ounces) frozen spinach, defrosted
> 3 tablespoons butter
> ½ cup finely chopped shallots
> ½ teaspoon dried thyme
> ½ teaspoon crumbled dried marjoram
> 1½ teaspoons salt
> ¼ teaspoon freshly ground black pepper
> ½ cup fresh bread crumbs (see Notes)
> 1 egg, lightly beaten
> 1 large onion
> 2 carrots
> 2 cups water

Preheat oven to 400° F.

Pat the boned meat dry with paper towels and set it aside. Reserve the bones.

Place the ground meats in a medium-sized mixing bowl and set aside. Place the defrosted spinach in a shallow dish. Tilting the dish over the sink, press the spinach with the palm of your hand and squeeze the liquid from it into the sink. When you have extracted as much of the liquid as you can, chop the spinach coarsely, and set it aside.

Melt the butter in a small heavy skillet over medium heat. When the butter is hot, stir in the shallots, then let them cook for 2 or 3 minutes, or until they are transparent. Add the chopped spinach; stirring with a wooden spoon, cook it until it is dry and sticks slightly to the bottom of the pan. *Remove the pan from heat.*

Add the spinach mixture to the ground meats in the bowl. Add the thyme, marjoram, salt, pepper to taste, bread crumbs, and beaten egg. Using a wooden spoon, mix the ingredients together until they are thoroughly combined. Pack the stuffing into the pocket in the breast of veal.

To keep the stuffing securely in the pocket while the meat roasts, tie it tightly closed with trussing cord. Tie the cord around the meat in 4 to 6 places, ending each tie with a double knot before cutting the cord.

Arrange the bones like a rack in a large roasting pan. Set the stuffed veal on the bones, add the onion and carrots to the pan, and cover tightly with aluminum foil. Place the casserole on the middle shelf of the oven and roast the veal, uncovered, for 30 minutes (set your timer).

Add the water to the pan, cover the casserole, and reduce oven heat to 350° F. Let the roast braise for 2 hours more (set your timer).

To test for doneness, insert the tip of a sharp knife into the thickest part of the meat. If the juices run clear with no trace of pink, the veal is done. If not, cover the casserole, let the veal roast for about 10 minutes longer and test again.

Transfer the veal to a heated large serving platter. Cut away and discard the trussing cords. Cover the roast loosely with aluminum foil and allow it to rest for 10 minutes before carving. While the roast rests, skim the fat from the juices in the pan. Taste for salt and pepper. Strain the juices into a heated sauceboat and serve with the meat.

NOTE:
Make the bread crumbs in an electric blender from 2 slices of fresh white bread with crusts removed.

SHOULDER LAMB CHOPS, MIDDLE EASTERN STYLE

(SERVES 6 TO 8)

> 2 tablespoons olive oil
> 8 shoulder lamb chops, trimmed of excess fat
> 1 teaspoon salt
> ¼ teaspoon freshly ground black pepper
> 1 to 1½ cups flour
> 1 tablespoon tomato paste
> 1½ cups water
> 1 large onion, sliced into thin rings
> 1 teaspoon finely chopped garlic (1 medium-sized clove)
> ½ teaspoon cuminseeds, pounded with a pestle in a mortar

Preheat oven to 425° F.

Pour the oil into a shallow roasting pan large enough to hold the chops in one layer so they will not touch each other. Place the pan of oil on the middle shelf of the oven.

While the oil heats (it will take about 10 minutes), salt and pepper the chops on both sides, dredge them with flour, and shake off any excess.

When the oil is hot, arrange the chops in the pan in one layer so as not to touch each other and bake them for 10 minutes (set your timer). Using a meat fork, tongs, or metal spatula, turn the chops over and let them bake for 10 minutes more (set your timer), or until they have lightly colored.

While the chops bake, thoroughly dissolve the tomato paste in the water. When the chops have colored lightly, scatter the onion rings over them, then the garlic, and sprinkle the top with the pounded cuminseeds. Pour the tomato liquid over, and *reduce oven heat to 350° F.*

Bake the chops, turning them over every 10 minutes or so, until most of the liquid has been absorbed and the chops have taken on a deep brown luster.

ROAST PORK WITH MUSTARD GLAZE

(SERVES 4 TO 6)

> 3 pounds center-cut pork loin
> 1 teaspoon salt
> 2 tablespoons Dijon mustard
> ¼ cup fresh bread crumbs (see Notes)
> 2 tablespoons chopped fresh parsley

Preheat oven to 350° F.

Place the loin of pork on a rack set in a roasting pan. Sprinkle the pork with the salt, and place the pan on the middle shelf of the oven. Roast the pork for 1 hour (set your timer).

Remove the pan from the oven. Let the pork rest on the rack; using a metal spatula, spread it with the Dijon mustard. Toss the bread crumbs and parsley together, then sprinkle the mixture on the mustard coating. Return the pork to the middle shelf of the oven and let it roast for 30 minutes (set your timer). (If you use a meat thermometer, be sure it is inserted into the thickest part of the pork, touching neither bone nor fat. When the thermometer reads 170° F., the roast is done.)

Transfer the roast to a carving board and let it rest for 10 minutes before serving.

NOTE:
Make bread crumbs in a blender from 1 slice of fresh bread without crusts.

ROAST FRESH HAM WITH BARBECUE SAUCE

When roasting a ham of this size it is best to use a thermometer to gauge doneness (170° F.). Before roasting, insert it into the thickest part of the meat, but not close to the bone. If you don't use a thermometer, count on 25 to 30 minutes per pound, and test for doneness as described in the recipe.

Basting with the sour-sweet barbecue sauce gives the ham a deep reddish-brown glaze. It's a great dish for a big dinner party: handsome to look at, rich-tasting, and juicy.

(SERVES 8 TO 10)

> *HAM*
> 1 whole fresh ham, 8 to 10 pounds
> 1 teaspoon salt
> Freshly ground black pepper
>
> *SAUCE*
> 2 tablespoons vegetable oil
> 1 cup finely chopped onion (1 large onion)
> 1½ cups tomato purée
> ½ cup water
> ¼ cup honey
> 2 tablespoons Worcestershire sauce
> 1½ teaspoons dry mustard
> 1 bay leaf
> ½ teaspoon salt
> 3 tablespoons wine vinegar

Preheat oven to 325° F.

Place the ham on a rack set in a shallow roasting pan. Sprinkle it with the salt and pepper, place it on the lower middle shelf of the oven, and roast for 3 hours.

SAUCE

Set a heavy 1-quart saucepan over medium heat, then add the oil. When the oil is very hot, stir in the onion and let it cook until lightly brown. Add the tomato purée, water, honey, Worcestershire sauce, dry mustard, bay leaf, and salt. Using a wooden spoon, stir all the ingredients together until well combined. Reduce heat and let the sauce simmer for 20 minutes (set your timer).

Strain the sauce through a fine sieve into a medium-sized heatproof bowl, pressing down on the solids to extract their juices. Discard the solids remaining in the sieve. Stir the vinegar into the sauce, and set the sauce aside.

When the ham has roasted for 3 hours, remove the pan from the oven, but do not turn oven off. Transfer the ham to a large platter. Discard all the fat remaining in the pan, then clean and dry the pan.

Remove the crackling, then trim the ham of all its fat. Return the ham to the rack set in the cleaned roasting pan. Using a large pastry brush, coat the entire surface of the ham with some of the sauce.

Return the ham to the lower middle shelf of the oven, and let it continue to roast for an additional hour (set your timer), brushing it with the sauce every 15 minutes or so. If you have used a thermometer, it will read 170° F. when the ham is done. If you have not used one, test for doneness by piercing the ham deeply in its thickest part with a paring knife. If it pierces easily, the ham is done. If it is resistant, let the ham roast for 15 minutes more (set your timer), and test again.

Transfer the ham to a large heated serving platter, cover it loosely with aluminum foil, and let it rest for 15 minutes before carving. Serve the remaining sauce in a heated sauceboat.

NOTES:
Leftover fresh ham, diced, is especially good in place of chicken in your favorite cold chicken salad.
Sliced thinly, leftover fresh ham is excellent for sandwiches.

BAKED HAM IN A PASTRY CAPE

Set on your buffet or dinner-party table, Baked Ham in a Pastry Cape is certain to be the star attraction. Each succulent slice—cut as thinly as you wish—will be edged with pungent, mustard-flavored pastry.

(SERVES 10 TO 12)

> *HAM*
> 1 precooked smoked ham, 12 to 14 pounds
> 1 large onion, sliced
> 1 bay leaf
> 1 celery rib
> 3 cloves
> ¼ cup Madeira
> 1 tablespoon arrowroot mixed with 1 tablespoon water
> Salt
> Pepper
> ¼ cup prepared mustard
>
> *PASTRY*
> 1 recipe Flaky Pastry (p. 25)
>
> *GLAZE*
> 1 egg yolk
> 2 tablespoons cream or milk

Preheat oven to 325° F.

With a small sharp knife, remove the rind from the ham. Reserve the rind.

Trim the ham of all but ¼ inch of its fat. Discard the excess fat. Set the ham in a large shallow roasting pan, place it on the middle shelf of the oven, and roast for 3 hours.

Place the ham rind in a 2-quart saucepan with cold water to cover. Add the onion slices, bay leaf, celery, and cloves, and bring the liquid to a boil over high heat. Reduce the heat and let the stock simmer for 45 minutes (set your timer).

Strain the stock through a sieve into a heatproof bowl. Discard the solids remaining in the sieve. Measure off 2 cups of the stock and set it aside. Discard remaining stock.

At the end of the roasting period, *turn off oven heat*. Remove the ham from the oven and let it cool in the roasting pan to room temperature. When the ham has cooled, transfer it to a large cookie sheet.

Pour off and discard all the fat remaining in the roasting pan. Pour the 2 cups of reserved stock into the pan, and set the pan over medium heat. With a metal spatula, scrape in any brown bits adhering to the bottom and sides of the pan, and cook until the stock is very hot. Pour in the Madeira, stir the arrowroot-water mixture to redissolve it, and add it to the pan. Reduce heat, and let the sauce simmer until slightly thickened, 6 to 8 minutes. Taste for salt and pepper, and set the sauce aside.

Using a metal spatula, spread the mustard on the top of the ham and halfway down the sides. Let the ham remain on the cookie sheet, and set it aside.

PASTRY CAPE

Preheat oven to 325° F.

Remove the pastry from the refrigerator, unwrap, and place it on a lightly floured surface. Lightly flour your rolling pin and the top of the pastry. Roll out the pastry into a circular shape, always rolling out from the center and ending each stroke just short of the edge so as not to thin out the edge too soon; you need a little thickness to hold when you turn it. Never roll back toward the center. Turn the pastry clockwise from time to time to test if it is sticking to the surface. If it sticks, flour lightly underneath. Continue rolling out the pastry until it is about ¼ inch in thickness. There will be enough pastry for the cape; decorations for the top can be cut from the excess.

Set the ham, still on its cookie sheet, alongside the rolled-out pastry. Place the rolling pin on the part of the pastry that is farthest from you. With the aid of a metal spatula, lift the far edge of the pastry onto the back of the rolling pin. Using your finger-tips, lightly press the pastry against the back of the rolling pin—

just enough to make it adhere—and roll the pastry toward yourself, making *1 complete turn.*

Lift the pastry-covered rolling pin by the handles, allowing the remainder of the pastry to hang down freely. Starting at one end of the ham, drape it with the pastry as you unroll it from the rolling pin. Mustard coats the ham halfway down the sides; using the mustard edge as a guide, trim the pastry with scissors into an oval shape. Gently press the pastry to the sides of the ham.

To decorate the top, roll out the excess pastry, and cut decorative shapes with a cookie cutter. Beat the egg yolk and the cream (or milk) together until well combined. With a pastry brush dipped into this mixture, dampen the underside of each shape and press it onto the pastry. Then brush a film of the mixture over the entire surface of the pastry.

Place the cookie sheet on the middle shelf of the oven and bake the ham for 45 minutes (set your timer), or until the pastry is deep gold.

NOTES:

When used for a buffet, Baked Ham in a Pastry Cape is served at room temperature and, therefore, unaccompanied by its sauce. Refrigerate the sauce and use it for reheating any of the leftover ham. Heat the sauce over low heat. Still over low heat, add the ham in slices, and simmer until heated through.

The ham bone is ideal for Green Split Pea Soup (p. 91). Wrapped so as to be airtight, it keeps safely in the freezer for up to 3 months.

You may like to try Cream Cheese Pastry (p. 24) in place of Flaky Pastry; its flavor complements that of ham.

STUFFED CABBAGE

(SERVES 4 TO 6)

1 large head of green cabbage, about 3½ pounds

FILLING
2 tablespoons butter
1 cup finely chopped onion (1 large onion)
1 teaspoon finely chopped garlic (1 medium-sized clove)
¼ pound pork ⎫
¼ pound beef ⎬ ground together
¼ pound veal ⎭
¾ cup cooked rice (¼ cup raw rice, cooked)
2 eggs (U.S. Graded Large)
1 teaspoon salt
½ teaspoon freshly ground black pepper
½ teaspoon crumbled dried marjoram

SAUCE
2 tablespoons butter
½ cup finely chopped onion
½ cup tomato purée
1½ cups chicken broth, homemade or canned
½ teaspoon sugar combined with ½ teaspoon freshly
    ground black pepper

Remove and discard any bruised leaves, then wash the head of cabbage under cold running water. Set a large pot of water over high heat, bring it to boil, then add the cabbage. After 6 minutes, remove the cabbage. Set it aside for a few minutes until it is cool enough to handle, then peel off outer leaves that come away easily, laying them out on paper towels to drain. Return the cabbage to the boiling water. Repeat the procedure as just described until you have peeled off 8 large leaves. Keep the remaining cabbage for some other use.

With a small sharp knife, remove the core from each leaf, cutting it out in a wedge shape. Discard the cores. Let the leaves continue to drain.

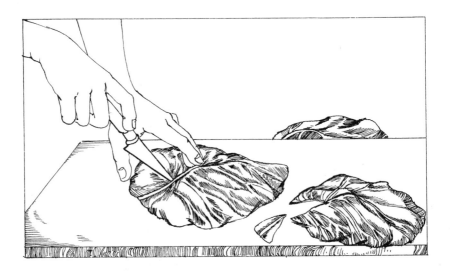

FILLING

Melt the butter in a 10-inch skillet over medium heat. When the butter is very hot, stir in the onion, and let it cook until transparent. Stir in the garlic, and let the mixture cook for 2 or 3 minutes more. Add the ground meats; using a wooden spoon, break up the lumps into small pieces. Stirring now and then, let the meat cook until it has browned.

Scrape the contents of the skillet into a medium-sized mixing bowl. Add the cooked rice, eggs, salt, pepper to taste, and marjoram, and mix the ingredients with a wooden spoon until thoroughly combined. Set aside.

SAUCE

Melt the butter in the same skillet over medium heat. When the butter is very hot, stir in the onion, and let it cook until lightly colored. Stir in the tomato purée, then the chicken broth, and reduce heat to low. Partially cover the skillet and let the sauce simmer for 20 minutes (set your timer).

Preheat oven to 350° F.

While the sauce cooks, fill the cabbage leaves. Lay out each leaf flat, wedge-cut edge nearest you, on the work surface. Equally distribute the meat mixture, centering a mound on each leaf.

Using both hands, lift the entire edge nearest you over the mixture. Bring the left side of the leaf over, then the right side. Now, roll the filled leaf over to form a tight packet completely enclosing the mixture. Repeat with the remaining leaves.

Spread one third of the sauce on the bottom of a shallow baking dish 10 × 14 × 2 inches. Arrange the packets, seam side down, on the sauce in one layer. Pour the remaining sauce over them. Sprinkle the top with the combined sugar and black pepper. Cover the dish tightly with aluminum foil, place it on the middle shelf of the oven, and bake for 45 minutes (set your timer).

When the timer bell rings, remove the foil, and bake until the sauce has reduced by half, about 30 minutes, basting the cabbage with the sauce from the casserole about every 10 minutes.

NOTE:

If you like, Stuffed Cabbage may be made 2 days ahead of time. Remove the casserole from the oven after it has baked for 45 minutes. Bring to room temperature, cover, then place it in the refrigerator. To finish the dish, uncover the casserole, set it on the middle shelf of a preheated 350° F. oven, and bake until the sauce has reduced by half, about 30 minutes.

Vegetables and Accompaniments

BAKED TOMATO HALVES

(SERVES 6)

        4 tablespoons butter
        2 tablespoons chopped shallots
        1 cup fresh bread crumbs (see Notes)
        ½ teaspoon crumbled dried basil
        2 tablespoons finely chopped fresh parsely
        ¼ teaspoon salt
        ¼ teaspoon freshly ground black pepper
        3 large tomatoes, approximately 1½ pounds
        Salt
        Pepper
        1½ teaspoons butter, in tiny bits

Preheat oven to 400° F.

Melt 1 tablespoon of the butter in a 10-inch skillet over medium heat. Using a wooden spoon, stir in the shallots; stirring con-

---

stantly, cook them until they are transparent. Transfer the shallots to a small bowl, and set aside.

Melt remaining 3 tablespoons of butter in the same skillet over medium heat. When the butter is very hot, add the bread crumbs; with a wooden spoon, stir them constantly as they toast, darkening evenly, to pale gold, 4 to 6 minutes.

Add the bread crumbs to the shallots in the bowl. Scatter the basil over the crumbs, then the parsley. Add 1/4 teaspoon salt and 1/4 teaspoon pepper, or more to taste. Toss all the ingredients together lightly, and set the bowl aside.

Wash and dry the tomatoes. Cut them horizontally into halves and season them lightly with salt and pepper. Grease a shallow ovenproof baking dish large enough to hold the tomatoes so that they are close but do not touch. Arrange the tomatoes in the dish. Evenly distributing the bread-crumb mixture, top each tomato half. Dot each topping with about 1/4 teaspoon of the butter bits.

Place the baking dish on the lower shelf of the oven and bake for 15 to 20 minutes (set your timer). Test for doneness by inserting the tips of fork tines into a side of each tomato. If the tomato has retained its shape but lost its firmness, it is done. If it is still firm, bake for a few minutes longer, and test again. Remove to serving dish with a large metal spatula.

NOTE:
Make the bread crumbs in an electric blender from 3 slices of fresh white bread with crusts removed.

BAKED ZUCCHINI

(SERVES 6)

> 3 tablespoons olive oil
> ½ cup chopped onion
> ½ teaspoon chopped garlic
> 2 cans (1 pound each) whole, solid-packed tomatoes
> 3 tablespoons tomato paste
> ½ teaspoon dried orégano
> 1 teaspoon crumbled dried basil
> 1 teaspoon salt
> ½ teaspoon freshly ground black pepper
> 2 pounds zucchini
> ½ cup freshly grated Parmesan cheese

Pour the olive oil into a 10- to 12-inch skillet over medium heat. When the oil is very hot, stir in the onion and let it cook until transparent. Stir in the garlic, and let it cook for 2 minutes. Add the tomatoes and all their liquid, then stir in the tomato paste, orégano, basil, salt, and pepper to taste. Raise heat to high and bring the liquid to a boil. Reduce heat, partially cover the skillet, and let the sauce simmer for 30 minutes (set your timer).

Bring 2 quarts of water to a boil over high heat. Meanwhile, scrub the zucchini clean under cold running water, then pat them dry with paper towels. Using a sharp knife, cut the zucchini into ½-inch-thick rounds. Add the zucchini rounds to the boiling water. When the water returns to boil, turn off heat, and drain the zucchini in a colander.

Preheat oven to 350° F.

Taste the cooked sauce for salt and pepper, then spread 1 cup of it on the bottom of a shallow baking dish 10 × 14 × 2 inches. Arrange a layer of zucchini rounds on the sauce, then spoon some of the remaining sauce over them. Cover with another layer of rounds, sauce it, and continue to make layers of rounds and sauce, ending with the sauce. Sprinkle the topmost sauced layer with all the grated Parmesan cheese. Place the dish on the middle shelf of the oven, and bake for 30 minutes (set your timer).

BRAISED CARROTS AND ONIONS

(SERVES 4 TO 6)

>1½ pounds small white onions, about 2 dozen
>6 medium-sized carrots
>½ teaspoon salt
>2 teaspoons sugar
>4 tablespoons butter
>¼ teaspoon freshly ground black pepper
>½ cup water

Preheat oven to 350° F.

Fill a large saucepan with about 8 cups of water and bring it to a boil over high heat. Add the onions, and bring the water back to a boil. Immediately drain the onions, and set them aside until cool enough to handle.

Meanwhile, scrape the carrots with a vegetable peeler, then, with a sharp knife, cut them diagonally into ¼-inch-thick slices. Peel the skins from the cooled onions.

Place the onions in a shallow casserole that has a tight-fitting cover. Add the carrots, salt, sugar, pepper to taste, and ½ cup water. Cover the casserole, or cover it tightly with aluminum foil, and place it on the middle shelf of the oven. Bake for 15 minutes (set your timer), then remove the cover and bake for 15 minutes more, or until the onions are tender and most of the water has evaporated.

᪣᪣«»᪣᪣

BRAISED LEEKS

Used as a vegetable to accompany a main dish, Braised Leeks are a pleasing surprise. Try them on their own as a first course, each serving sprinkled with chopped fresh parsley. Braised leeks accompanied by poached eggs make a marvelous main dish for brunch.

(SERVES 6)

> 6 leeks, each approximately 1½ inches in diameter
> 2 cups chicken broth, homemade or canned
> 4 tablespoons unsalted butter, cut into small pieces
> Freshly ground black pepper

Preheat oven to 350° F.

Follow the instructions for trimming and washing the leeks on page 85. *Do not slice them;* keep each leek in one piece about 6 inches long. Pare away and discard the thin, tough bottoms.

In a heavy shallow casserole, 10 × 14 × 2 inches, line up the leeks side by side in a row. Add the broth to the casserole, scatter the pieces of butter over the leeks, and sprinkle with pepper to taste.

Cover the casserole tightly with aluminum foil, place it on the middle shelf of the oven, and braise for 1 hour (set your timer).

Remove the foil, *raise oven heat to 450° F.,* and cook for 15 minutes (set your timer).

Turn the leeks over with tongs, and let them cook for 15 minutes more (set your timer). Test for doneness by inserting the tip of a sharp knife into the root end of one leek. If it pierces easily, all the leeks are done.

❧«»❦

BRAISED ENDIVE

(SERVES 6)

> 10 medium-sized endives
> ½ cup water
> 1 tablespoon fresh lemon juice
> 1 tablespoon Japanese soy sauce
> 4 tablespoons unsalted butter
> ½ teaspoon sugar
> 2 tablespoons chopped fresh parsley

Preheat oven to 375° F.

Using a small sharp knife, trim away any brown spots from the base of the endives. Wash the outer leaves of each endive under cold running water, pat them dry with paper towels, and arrange them in one layer in a shallow baking dish, about 12 × 16 inches, that has a tight-fitting cover.

Pour the water into a small saucepan, add the lemon juice, soy sauce, butter, and sugar, and bring the mixture to a boil over medium heat. When the butter has melted, pour the mixture over the endives. Cover the baking dish, or cover it tightly with aluminum foil, and place it on the middle shelf of the oven. Bake for 20 minutes (set your timer).

Remove the cover and bake for 15 minutes more (set your timer). Test for doneness by inserting the tip of a sharp knife in the thickest part of an endive. If there is no resistance to the knife, the endives are done. If they are not done, cover and bake for a few minutes longer, then test again.

RED CABBAGE

(SERVES 6)

> 1 head of red cabbage, about 3 pounds
> 2 tablespoons butter or bacon fat
> ¼ cup chopped onion
> 2 tart apples, pared, cored, and cut into ½-inch dice
> 3 tablespoons wine vinegar
> 1 tablespoon sugar
> 1 teaspoon salt
> 1 cup water

Preheat oven to 325° F.

Remove any bruised leaves from the cabbage and discard them. Wash the head of cabbage under cold running water, then pat it dry with paper towels. Quarter it with a sharp knife, then cut out and discard the core. One at a time, lay each quarter on one flat side and shred it thinly.

Over medium heat, melt the butter or bacon fat in a 4- to 6-quart casserole that has a tight-fitting cover. When the fat is very hot, stir in the onion and let it cook until lightly browned. Add the cabbage, apples, vinegar, sugar, salt, and water. Mix all the ingredients together, then remove the casserole from the heat.

Cut a circle of wax or parchment paper large enough to fit into the casserole. Press it down into the casserole and onto the cabbage mixture. Cover the casserole, place it on the middle shelf of the oven, and braise for 1½ hours (set your timer), or until the cabbage is very soft. As the cabbage braises, check it from time to time; if it seems dry, add ¼ cup of water.

NOTE:

Leftover red cabbage will lose its color while stored in the refrigerator. To bring it back to its original color, stir in 1 or 2 tablespoons of red-wine vinegar while reheating it.

BROCCOLI MOLD

Made this way, broccoli remains bright green and retains its natural flavor. Light and delicate, Broccoli Mold is no Monday-Night fare—it's definitely dinner-party food.

(SERVES 6 TO 8)

> 2½ pounds fresh broccoli (2 medium-sized bunches)
> 3½ teaspoons salt
> 2 teaspoons softened butter
> 4 eggs (U.S. Graded Large)
> ¼ teaspoon freshly ground black pepper
> ¼ cup heavy cream
> ¼ teaspoon freshly grated nutmeg

Fill an 8- to 10-quart pot with 6 quarts of water and bring it to a boil over high heat. Add 2 teaspoons of the salt, then the broccoli, and cook for 15 minutes (set your timer), or until it is tender. Set a colander in the sink, drain the broccoli in it, and let it cool to room temperature.

Preheat oven to 350° F.

Grease the entire inside of a 4-cup ring mold with the 2 teaspoons softened butter, and set it aside.

Chop the cooled broccoli very fine. Set a food mill (see Note) over a medium-sized bowl and purée the broccoli through it into the bowl. Beat the eggs, one at a time, thoroughly into the purée. Continuing to beat, add the remaining 1½ teaspoons salt, the pepper, heavy cream, and nutmeg until all the ingredients are well blended. Spoon the purée into the greased mold, cover it with a piece of buttered wax paper, buttered side down, and set it aside.

Bring a pan of water to a boil over high heat. When the water is boiling, set the covered ring mold in a roasting pan. Pull out the middle shelf of the oven and place the roasting pan on it. Pour enough of the boiling water into the pan to come at least halfway up the sides of the ring mold. Gently slide the shelf back into the oven, and bake for 30 minutes (set your timer).

Test for doneness by inserting a knife into the broccoli. If it comes out clean, the broccoli is done. If not, let it bake for a few minutes more and test again.

To unmold the broccoli, invert a warmed large, round serving plate on top of the mold. Using both hands, clamp plate and mold together and turn them over.

NOTE:
If you have an electric food processor, purée the chopped broccoli in it.

CORN CUSTARD WITH GREEN CHILIES

(SERVES 6)

> 1 tablespoon softened butter
> 1 can (4 ounces) whole green chilies
> 4 eggs (U.S. Graded Large)
> 1½ teaspoons salt
> 1½ cups milk
> 2 tablespoons grated onion
> 1 can (12-ounce) whole-kernel corn
> ¼ cup freshly grated Parmesan cheese

Grease the entire inside of a casserole 7 × 12 inches and 1½ inches deep with the softened butter, and set it aside.

Preheat oven to 350° F.

Drain the chilies and rinse them clean under cold running water. Slit each one down the side with a small sharp knife, and spread them flat. Scrape away the seeds. Chop the chilies coarsely and put them in a large mixing bowl. Add the eggs, salt, milk, grated onion, and corn. Beat the ingredients together with a fork until they are well combined.

Pour the mixture into the casserole; with a rubber spatula scrape out any chilies clinging to the sides of the bowl and add them to the casserole. Sprinkle the top with the grated Parmesan cheese, and place the casserole on the middle shelf of the oven. Bake for 30 minutes (set your timer), or until the custard has set. Test for doneness by inserting a knife into the custard. If the knife comes out clean, the custard has set. If not, bake a little longer, and test again.

❧«»☙

SPINACH SOUFFLÉ

(SERVES 4 TO 6)

> 1 package (10 ounces) frozen spinach, cooked
> 1 tablespoon butter (for greasing soufflé dish)
> 4 tablespoons butter
> 2 tablespoons finely chopped onion
> 4 tablespoons flour
> 1 cup milk
> ½ teaspoon salt
> ¼ teaspoon white pepper
> ¼ teaspoon freshly grated nutmeg
> 4 egg yolks (U.S. graded, large)
> 6 egg whites
> 2 tablespoons grated Parmesan cheese

Preheat oven to 400° F.

When you have cooked and drained the spinach, let it cool in a shallow dish. Tilting the dish of cooled spinach over the sink, press the spinach with the palm of your hand and squeeze the liquid from it into the sink. When you have extracted as much of the liquid as you can, chop the spinach and set it aside.

With 1 tablespoon butter, grease the entire inside of a 2-quart soufflé dish and set it aside.

Melt 4 tablespoons butter in a heavy 1-quart saucepan over low heat. When the butter is very hot, stir in the onion and let it cook until transparent. Add the flour, stirring it in with a wooden spoon until the mixture is smooth, and allow it to cook for 2 to 3 minutes. *Remove from the heat.*

Gradually add the milk, beating it into the mixture with a wire whisk. Return the saucepan to high heat and let the sauce come to a boil. Immediately, turn down the heat, add the salt, white pepper, and nutmeg, and simmer the sauce for 5 minutes (set your timer). *Remove from heat.*

One at a time, beat in the egg yolks with a wire whisk until well blended with the sauce. Stir in the spinach, and set the mixture aside.

Using a balloon whisk or an electric mixer, beat the egg whites in a large bowl until they form soft peaks. Stir one third of the egg whites into the spinach mixture. Pour the spinach mixture over the remaining egg whites, using a rubber spatula to scrape out all of the mixture that clings to the sides of the saucepan. Still using the rubber spatula, gently fold the egg whites and spinach together until no egg white shows. Work with a light touch so as not to reduce the volume.

Pour the mixture into the buttered soufflé dish, scraping into it any that clings to the sides of the bowl. Sprinkle the top with the grated Parmesan cheese and place the soufflé on the middle shelf of the oven. *Reduce heat to 375° F.*

Bake the soufflé for 30 minutes (set your timer). At the end of 30 minutes, the soufflé will have puffed up 2 to 3 inches above the edge of the dish, and the cheese will have turned to a delicate golden crust. The center of the soufflé will be slightly runny in texture, creating its own sauce. If you prefer a drier soufflé, *reduce heat to 350° F.* and bake it for 10 to 15 minutes more.

NEVER-STICK POTATOES ANNA

There are several variations on traditional French Potatoes Anna. This is the most glamorous-looking one; turned out of the skillet in which it bakes, the top is petaled and golden brown. Any truth-telling cook will admit to last-minute trepidations about unmolding the beautiful construction: will it slip smoothly onto the serving plate? Or will it stick to the pan? If it sticks, it's no longer glamorous; it's as simple as that.

The use of parchment paper to line the skillet prevents sticking. If you organize your small battery of utensils so they are near at hand, you can enjoy making the dish from beginning to end. You will need a vegetable scraper, a large bowl of cold water, kitchen or baker's parchment paper, scissors, a pastry brush, a good sharp knife, and an 8-inch heavy skillet with a heat-resistant handle.

(SERVES 4 TO 6)

> ¼ pound unsalted butter (1 stick)
> 3½ to 4 pounds baking potatoes
> 1 tablespoon salt
> 2 teaspoons freshly ground black pepper

Melt the butter in a small saucepan over low heat. Set it aside. As you peel each potato with the vegetable scraper, immediately place it in the bowl of cold water. Set the bowl of potatoes aside and proceed with making the parchment paper lining for the 8-inch skillet.

Measure off a length of parchment paper about 1 inch longer than needed to cover the top of the skillet. Cut it off evenly. Fold it exactly in half. Fold it in half again to form a square. Fold the square in half to form a triangle. Fold the triangle in half to form a pointed cone.

Take hold of the cone, about 1 inch from its tip, between the thumb and index finger of your left hand. Palm up, hold the tip over dead center of the bottom of the skillet. Lower the wide

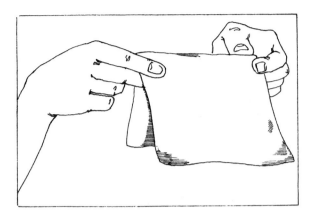

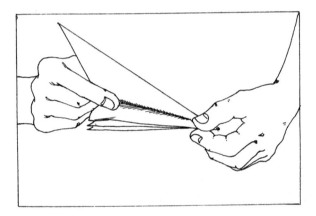

end to the rim of the skillet. With your right hand, press opened scissors against the outer rim of the skillet and, using the contour of the skillet as a guide, cut off the wide end of the paper that extends beyond the rim of the skillet.

Open the parchment cone: it will be a circle large enough to cover the bottom of the skillet and come up the sides about 1 inch. Set the lining aside.

Using a pastry brush, apply melted butter to the entire inside of the skillet. Center the paper lining in the skillet and press to make

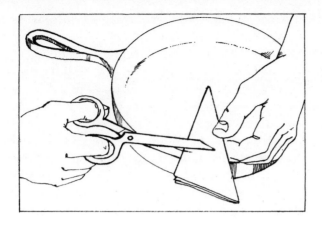

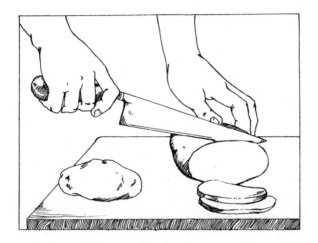

it adhere to the bottom and about 1 inch up all around the sides. Brush all of the paper lining with melted butter. Once more, brush melted butter on the exposed sides of the skillet above the paper lining. Set the skillet aside.

Preheat oven to 400° F.

One at a time, remove a potato from the cold water as you need it. Pat it dry with paper towels. Place it on your work surface so that its long side faces you horizontally. Starting from the back of the potato, cut off a slice about ½ inch thick. (Set this first slice aside for another purpose, or discard.) Continue to cut the potato into long slices $\frac{1}{16}$ inch thick.

On the bottom of the lined skillet, begin to lay out a centerpiece of long slices to look like petals, each one slightly overlapping. Add to the petals by slicing another potato as just described, until the centerpiece is completed.

All the petals laid out, now line the sides of the pan. Again, place a patted-dry potato to lie on the work surface horizontally. This time, cut off and set aside (or discard) the rounded ends. Cut rounds $\frac{1}{16}$ inch thick. Stand the rounds against the sides of the skillet, each one slightly overlapping. When the entire inner rim of the skillet is ringed by overlapping rounds, your pattern is fully designed. Dip your pastry brush in the melted butter and dribble some over the petals. Sprinkle the petals with $\frac{1}{4}$ teaspoon of the salt, and add a generous grinding of black pepper.

From now on, you can cut the potatoes any way you like, but be sure to slice them thinly. Build layers of potato slices, dribbling each finished layer with melted butter, then seasoning it with some of the salt and a generous grinding of pepper.

Ideally, the final layer should be flush with the top of the rounds lining the sides of the skillet. Your dish will be very successful even if it falls short of this ideal, but remember to dribble butter over the topmost layer, then sprinkle it with seasonings.

Cover the skillet tightly with aluminum foil. Place it on the middle shelf of the oven. *Set your timer for 45 minutes.*

At the end of this baking time, remove the foil from the skillet. *Set your timer for 30 minutes, and bake for 30 minutes more.*

Remove the skillet from the oven. Turn the potatoes out of the skillet by first running the end of a sharp knife (or the edge of a metal spatula) between the potato rounds and the sides of the pan. Shake the pan to be sure the rounds are completely loosened from the sides. Place an inverted 10-inch plate over the top of the skillet. With a potholder in each hand, hold plate and skillet together tightly and turn them over. Lift the skillet. If the paper lining still lies on the potatoes, remove it and discard. Serve Potatoes Anna hot.

POTATOES SOUBISE

Baked potatoes stuffed American-style require puréeing the potatoes, then combining them with other ingredients to achieve a
smooth, homogeneously textured and flavored dish. The character
of Potatoes Soubise is just the reverse: each ingredient is calculated
to retain its identity. Coarsely mashed potatoes are lightly mixed
into the French onion sauce, *soubise*. The proof of this dish is,
literally, in the eating. You will not only taste potato, onion bits,
pepper, nutmeg, and cheese, but savor each interesting texture.

(SERVES 6)

> 3 large baking potatoes
> 4 tablespoons butter
> ½ cup finely chopped onion
> 4 tablespoons flour
> 1 cup milk
> ½ teaspoon salt
> ¼ teaspoon freshly ground black pepper
> ¼ teaspoon grated nutmeg
> 2 tablespoons freshly grated Parmesan cheese

Preheat oven to 375° F.

Scrub each potato under cold running water until the skin is
clean, then dry well with paper towels. Place them on the middle
shelf of the oven and bake for 45 minutes (set your timer).

Melt the butter in a 1-quart heavy saucepan over low heat. As
soon as it melts, add the onion and cook for about 10 minutes, or
until soft, but do not let onion brown. Add the flour, stirring it in
with a wooden spoon until the mixture is smooth, and allow it to
cook for 2 to 3 minutes. *Remove from heat.*

Gradually add the milk, beating it into the onion-flour mixture
with a wire whisk. Stir in the salt, pepper, and nutmeg. Return the
pan to the heat, and let the sauce simmer for about 5 minutes. *Remove from heat*, and set it aside.

Remove the baked potatoes from oven and set them aside to

cool. Turn oven off. When cool enough to handle, cut the potatoes lengthwise into halves. Without breaking the skins, remove the meat of the potato with a soup spoon, scooping it out directly into the sauce. Arrange the skins, open side up on a baking sheet. Break up the potato in the sauce with a wire whisk, then spoon the mixture into the skins. Sprinkle each one with the grated Parmesan cheese.

At 45 minutes before serving time, preheat oven to 350° F.

Place the baking sheet of filled potatoes on the middle shelf of the oven and bake for 30 minutes (set your timer), or until the potatoes are very hot and the cheese has melted to crusty golden brown.

NOTE:
After the potato skins are filled they will keep safely at room temperature for 3 to 4 hours before finishing in the oven.

POTATO CHEESE CASSEROLE

Like potato salad, Potato Cheese Casserole tastes just as good served hot or at room temperature. If you like it at room temperature, you can bake it 2 hours ahead of time and simply set it aside.

(SERVES 6)

> 2 tablespoons butter
> 1½ cups grated Swiss cheese
> 2½ pounds boiling potatoes
> ½ teaspoon salt (depending on saltiness of broth)
> ½ teaspoon freshly grated black pepper
> 2 teaspoons finely chopped garlic (2 medium-sized cloves)
> 1 cup chicken broth, homemade or canned
> 1½ cups heavy cream

Preheat oven to 350° F.

With 1 tablespoon of the butter, grease a shallow baking dish 7 × 12 inches.

Set aside ¾ cup of the cheese for topping.

Peel the potatoes, then cut them into slices ¼ inch thick. Lay out enough to make one layer on the bottom of the buttered baking dish. Sprinkle them with a little of the salt and pepper, then with a little of the garlic and some of the cheese. Continue to make layers as just described until all the potatoes are used.

Top the final layer with the reserved ¾ cup cheese, distributing it evenly. Dot the topping with the remaining 1 tablespoon butter. Set the dish on a jelly-roll pan. First pour the broth over the topping, then the cream. Place the jelly-roll pan on the middle shelf of the oven and bake the potatoes for 1 hour (set your timer), or until the top is golden brown. Test for doneness by inserting the tip of a sharp knife through the potato layers. If there is no resistance to the knife, the potatoes are done.

RICE PILAF

(SERVES 4 TO 6)

> 2 tablespoons butter
> 1/4 cup chopped onion
> 1 cup uncooked rice
> 2 cups chicken broth, homemade or canned
> 1/4 cup dried currants
> Salt, depending on saltiness of broth
> 1/4 cup pistachio nuts, shelled
> 1/2 teaspoon freshly ground black pepper

Preheat oven to 350° F.

Over medium heat, melt the butter in a 1-quart casserole that has a tight-fitting cover. When the butter is very hot, stir in the onion and let it cook until golden. Add the rice and stir it in until each grain is entirely coated with butter.

Pour in the chicken broth, add the currants, then taste for salt. Bring the mixture to a boil over high heat. *Immediately remove from heat, and cover the casserole.* Place it on the middle shelf of the oven and bake for 25 minutes (set your timer), or until all the liquid has been absorbed.

While the rice bakes, blanch the shelled pistachio nuts by dropping them into boiling water. After 15 seconds, drain them through a fine-meshed strainer. Place the nuts on a kitchen towel, fold the towel over them and, with the palm of your hand, roll the nuts back and forth to remove their skins. Use a sharp knife to scrape off any bits of skin that may remain. Discard the skins. Chop the skinned nuts coarsely, and set them aside.

Remove the casserole from oven. With a fork lightly stir the nuts and pepper through the rice.

NOTE:
It's important to stir the rice into the onion-butter mixture until all the rice kernels are coated with butter. The purpose of this is to keep the rice from sticking together.

BARLEY CASSEROLE

Soups made with barley are so delicious, we rarely think of using the grain in any other way. Here's a suggestion: when you find yourself thinking *rice? potatoes?* to accompany a main dish, it's time to make the Barley Casserole. To savor fully its distinct mushroom flavor, don't make the mistake of serving it along with another mushroom-flavored dish.

(SERVES 6)

> 2 tablespoons butter
> 2 tablespoons chopped shallots
> 1/4 pound fresh mushrooms, finely chopped
> 1 cup medium pearled barley
> 2 to 2 1/2 cups chicken broth, homemade or canned
> Salt, depending on saltiness of broth
> 1/4 teaspoon freshly ground black pepper
> 1/4 cup thinly sliced scallions, green part included
> 2 tablespoons chopped fresh parsley

Preheat oven to 350° F.

Over medium heat, melt the butter in a 2-quart casserole that has a tight-fitting cover. When the butter is hot, stir in the shallots and let them cook until they are transparent. Add the mushrooms and cook them until they are soft. Stir the barley into the mixture, pour in 2 cups of the chicken broth, and add salt and pepper to taste. Bring the mixture to a boil over high heat. *Immediately, remove from heat.*

Cover the casserole, place it on the middle shelf of the oven, and bake for 45 minutes (set your timer), or until all the broth has been absorbed and the barley is tender. If the barley looks too dry, add the other 1/2 cup broth, cover the casserole, and bake for 15 minutes longer.

Remove the casserole from oven. With a fork, lightly stir the scallions and parsley through the barley. Serve from the casserole.

Desserts

ALMOND CAKE

This remarkable French pastry is an example of one surprise after another. It may find a place at the top of your list of favorite cakes to bake. When the cake goes into the oven, it's almost flat; when it comes out, it has turned to crisp, flaky layers 2½ to 3 inches high. A design of lines etched on top of the cake spreads apart while baking, to show pale petal forms against a dark-gold background.

Almond Cake is based on a traditional specialty made in Pithiviers, the Loire Valley town famed for its almond-flavored pastries. This cake, like the traditional one, is constructed of two layers of puff pastry, but the texture of the almond filling differs from the original—it's moister because of the addition of canned almond paste. The fresh flavor of lemon has also been added to the traditional hint of rum.

(SERVES 8 TO 10)

½ recipe Puff Pastry (p. 30)
1¼ cups almonds, blanched and toasted
¼ cup canned almond paste
4 tablespoons unsalted butter
3 egg yolks
½ teaspoon vanilla extract
1 teaspoon freshly grated lemon rind
2 tablespoons dark rum
½ cup confectioners' sugar

Remove the puff pastry from the refrigerator. Unwrap, and place it on a lightly floured surface. With a sharp knife, cut it into 2 pieces equal in size. Wrap each piece loosely in wax paper, and return them to the refrigerator.

FILLING

Pulverize the almonds, one third at a time, in the container of an electric blender set at high speed. Dump each pulverized batch into a large mixing bowl.

Scrape the almond paste into the bowl, then add the butter, egg yolks, vanilla, grated lemon rind, and rum. Using a wooden spoon, beat the ingredients together to blend them thoroughly, and continue beating until the mixture forms a mass thick enough for the spoon to stand upright in it. Set the almond mixture aside.

PASTRY

Remove 1 piece of the puff pastry from the refrigerator, unwrap, and place it on a lightly floured surface. Lightly flour your rolling pin and the surface of the pastry, and roll the pastry into a square. Evenly distributing your weight on the handles of the rolling pin, roll it on the pastry all the way to the edges—first away from yourself, then back toward yourself. To test for sticking, run a metal spatula underneath the pastry. If it sticks, dust lightly underneath with flour. Continue rolling until it is a 9-inch square.

Invert an 8-inch circular plate on the 9-inch square of pastry.

With a sharp knife, and using the rim of the plate as a guide, cut out a disc of pastry.

Run cold water over a large cookie sheet, shake off the excess, and set the cookie sheet on the work surface. With your fingers and the aid of a metal spatula, gently lift the disc of pastry and center it on the cookie sheet. Using an icing spatula, spread the almond mixture evenly on the pastry, leaving a ½-inch pastry border exposed around the entire disc. Set the cookie sheet aside.

Remove the remaining piece of pastry from the refrigerator, unwrap, and place it on a lightly floured surface. Roll it out exactly as just described, but this time into a 10-inch square. Invert a 9-inch circular plate on the 10-inch square of pastry. Again using the rim of the plate as a guide, cut out a disc of pastry.

Dip a pastry brush lightly into cold water, then dampen the exposed border of the first disc. Lift the second disc as you did before —gently, and with the aid of a metal spatula—and set it on top of the filling so the edges of both pastry discs meet evenly. With the tips of your fingers, lightly press top and bottom borders of pastry together.

Setting the back of the blade of a small knife against the border of pastry, make straight, up-and-down, ¼-inch-deep indentations, about 1 inch apart, all around the edge.

Place the cookie sheet in the refrigerator, then *set your timer for 15 minutes*. When the timer bell rings, *preheat oven to 425° F.* Then *reset your timer for 15 minutes* to be sure the cake has chilled for at least 30 minutes. Remove the cookie sheet from the refrigerator and set it on the work surface. Cut a vent in the top center of the cake: with a small sharp knife, or with a 1-inch round cookie cutter, cut out a circle of pastry about 1 inch in diameter.

Designing the top of the cake

Visualize the cake as the face of a clock. About ½ inch in from the outer edge and all around the clock, mark it with the tip of a sharp knife. Mark it at 12 o'clock, 3 o'clock, 6 o'clock, and 9 o'clock, then mark it midway between each of these points. There will be 8 marks at equal intervals.

To incise the design, hold the small sharp knife properly. Blade down, hold the whole handle firmly in your palm, thumb securely on the handle at the base close to the blade. Tighten your fingers around the handle, making a fist. Rotate your wrist to the right until your fist is sideways and the knife blade at an angle.

The design consists of an elongated ſ, incised 4 times about ⅛ inch deep, spanning the top of the cake, but skipping over the vent. Begin incising the first elongated ſ slightly to the right of the mark at 12 o'clock, skip over the vent, and continue the ſ, ending

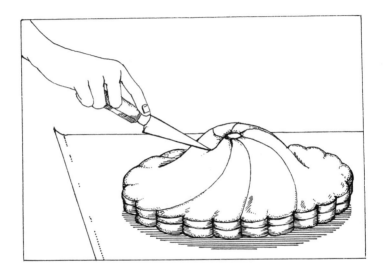

slightly to the left of the mark at 6 o'clock. When skipping over the vent, sustain the movement of making the elongated ſ by rotating your wrist slightly to the left, then back to the fist-sideways position to incise the lower reverse curve.

Turning the cake counterclockwise so as to incise the ſ each time from the position at 12 o'clock, repeat the design 3 times more as just described. You will end with 8 curves which seem to be moving in the same direction, as in a wheel.

Set the cookie sheet on the middle shelf of the oven and bake the cake 10 minutes (set your timer). Reduce oven heat to 375° F., and bake for 20 minutes more (set your timer), or until the cake is deep gold.

Remove the cookie sheet from oven. *Increase heat to 500° F.* Hold a sieve over the cake, shaking the sieve as you dump the confectioners' sugar into it. Continue to shake it, covering the whole top of the cake with all of the sugar. Return the cookie sheet to the middle shelf of the oven, and bake the cake for 5 minutes (set your timer), or until the sugar has melted and caramelized.

Remove the cookie sheet from the oven. With the aid of a metal spatula, slide the cake from the cookie sheet onto a wire rack to cool to room temperature.

CHEESECAKE

To find a superb cheesecake in a bakery is rare; for most commercial establishments, the cost of ingredients alone is prohibitive. If you really love cheesecake, the best one you'll ever have is the one you make at home.

The commercial variety is often dry and has a thick unpalatable crust. A good one is very moist and creamy. To achieve the proper consistency, cream cheese is an essential ingredient. For the following recipe 2 cups of sour cream are needed as well. Most commercial bakers use inferior substitutes, but if you've bought one and think it's great, try this recipe once. The chances are you'll never buy another.

(SERVES 8 TO 10)

> CRUST
> 1 tablespoon unsalted butter, softened
> 1 cup graham cracker crumbs (see Notes)
> 3 tablespoons sugar
> ½ teaspoon ground cinnamon
> 4 tablespoons unsalted butter, melted and cooled to
>   room temperature

Preheat oven to 350° F.

With 1 tablespoon softened butter, grease the whole inside of a springform pan 9 × 3 inches. Set it aside.

Place the crumbs, sugar, cinnamon, and 4 tablespoons butter in a small bowl; using a wooden spoon, combine them until thoroughly blended.

Measure off ¾ cup of the crumb mixture to line the pan, and set the remainder aside for topping the baked cake.

Press the mixture into the buttered bottom and sides of the pan, making the bottom crust twice as thick as that on the sides. Place the pan in the refrigerator to chill the crust while you make the filling.

FILLING

3 packages (8 ounces each) cream cheese, at room
    temperature
1¼ cups sugar
6 eggs (U.S. Graded Large), separated
⅓ cup all-purpose flour
2 cups sour cream
2 teaspoons vanilla extract
1 tablespoon grated lemon rind
2 tablespoons fresh lemon juice

Place the cream cheese in a large mixing bowl. Using either a wooden spoon or an electric mixer set on low speed, beat the cheese until it is soft. Add the sugar gradually, beating it in until the mixture is light and fluffy. One at a time, beat in the egg yolks, beating each one in until well blended with the mixture. Using a wooden spoon, stir in the flour, then the sour cream, vanilla, lemon rind, and lemon juice. Continue stirring until the texture is smooth.

Beat the egg whites with an electric mixer until they hold stiff peaks. With a rubber spatula, add about one third of the beaten whites to the cheese mixture, stirring them together thoroughly. Pour this mixture into the remaining egg whites; still using the rubber spatula, fold them together. Fold quickly and thoroughly, but with a light touch so as not to decrease the volume of the egg whites.

Remove the springform pan from the refrigerator. Pour the filling into the pan, using the rubber spatula to get all of it. Place the pan on the middle shelf of the oven and bake for 1 hour and 15 minutes (set your timer), or until the top is golden. Turn off the oven heat, and let the cake cool in the oven for 1 hour.

Remove from the oven to a wire rack. Let the cake cool in its pan to room temperature.

Sprinkle the reserved crumb mixture over the top of the cake. Place cake in the refrigerator to chill in its pan for at least 3 hours. Just before serving, sift confectioners' sugar over the top.

NOTES:
REFRIGERATOR STORAGE: Safe for 3 to 4 days, tightly enclosed with plastic wrap. *Do not freeze.*
To make graham cracker crumbs, place crackers in a paper bag and crush with a rolling pin.

LEMON DACQUOISE

With lemon buttercream in place of one flavored with coffee, this *dacquoise* is the same cake described in the Christmas issue of *The New Yorker* in 1959 by the distinguished food editor, the late Sheila Hibben. She referred to it as "a specialty of Mr. Clancy's" —which it was, and is—recommending it to her readers as "fragile and light as a feather." Unable to give the history or background of the dish, she explained that she had never heard of it before, nor had any of her "usual dependable culinary authorities." John Clancy's anecdote will clear up for culinary history fans the mystery of how the dessert found its way from France to New York City, and perhaps to all of America.

"Before leaving New York City for my summer job as chef at Chillingsworth on Cape Cod, I always paid Jim Beard an annual farewell visit. Jim was the food consultant for Chillingsworth; we worked closely on new menu ideas.

"I remember that day in the spring of 1959. When I arrived, Jim was reading a French food magazine. Without looking up, without greeting me, he said, 'Listen, John, there's something in here called *dacquoise*. I've never heard of it before, but it sounds like a marvelous idea for Chillingsworth.' Translating from the French, he reeled off the ingredient list, and I wrote it down. I can still recall how excited we were as he translated the technique for what turned out to be ground-almond-filled meringues, and then the coffee buttercream to hold them together.

"I tested the recipe as soon as I got to Chillingsworth, then tried it out at the tasting party for the press. It was a smash! I put it on the summer menu: instant success! Believe it or not, it still is.

"It was in the fall of '59 that Sheila Hibben telephoned Jim in her search for new food ideas in preparation for the Christmas issue. Jim said, 'Call John Clancy. He makes a beautiful dessert called *dacquoise*. I'm sure he'll make one for you.'

"Later, when I was chef at the Coach House, I put it on their menu. After I left, they kept it on. Craig Claiborne came in and tasted it, then devoted a whole *New York Times* (Sunday) *Magazine* article to the recipe, along with a rave review."

The version in the French magazine called for baking the

meringues in flan rings, but using layer-cake pans—as in this recipe—makes them more controllable. The meringue layers can be very chewy or very crisp. In this recipe, they are chewy; if you prefer them crisp, make them 3 to 4 days in advance. If you live in a dry climate, put them in an airtight container and keep them at room temperature. In a humid climate, it's safest to put them into plastic bags first, then into the airtight container.

(SERVES 6 TO 8)

>2 teaspoons softened butter
>2 tablespoons flour
>
>*MERINGUES*
>1 cup unsalted whole almonds, blanched and toasted
>2/3 cup granulated sugar
>2 tablespoons cornstarch
>6 egg whites (U.S. Graded Large)
>
>*LEMON BUTTERCREAM*
>3 egg yolks (U.S. Graded Large)
>1 cup confectioners' sugar
>1/2 cup hot milk
>1/2 pound (2 sticks) unsalted butter, cold
>1 tablespoon fresh lemon juice
>2 tablespoons freshly grated lemon rind
>1 cup heavy cream, whipped, refrigerated
>
>1/2 cup unsalted toasted almonds, sliced
>1/4 cup confectioners' sugar, sifted

Preheat oven to 325° F.

Prepare two 9-inch layer-cake pans. Using 1 teaspoon of the softened butter for each one, grease the entire inside of the pans. Dump 1 tablespoon of flour into each pan. Toss it about to coat the entire inside of the pan, then shake out the excess. Set the pans aside.

MERINGUES

Pulverize the whole almonds, one third at a time, in the container of an electric blender on high speed, transferring them as they are grated to a small bowl.

Add the sugar and cornstarch to all of the grated almonds; using a fork, stir the ingredients together until thoroughly combined.

In a large bowl, beat the egg whites with an electric mixer until they hold stiff peaks. Sprinkle the nut mixture over the egg whites; using a rubber spatula, gently fold the ingredients together. Still using the rubber spatula, divide the mixture evenly into the 2 prepared layer-cake pans, smoothing the tops.

Place the pans on the middle shelf of the oven and bake the meringues for 1 hour and 15 minutes (set your timer), or until the layers are pale brown and have shrunk slightly from the edges of the pans.

Remove the pans from the oven, turn the meringues out onto wire racks, and let them cool to room temperature. Meanwhile, prepare the lemon buttercream.

LEMON BUTTERCREAM

Put the egg yolks in a heavy enamelware saucepan, then add 1 cup confectioners' sugar all at once. Using a wooden spoon, mix the ingredients together until they turn to a smooth paste. Stirring constantly with the spoon, gradually add the hot milk. Continuing to stir, cook the mixture over medium heat until it lightly coats the spoon. *Do not let it come to a boil or it will curdle.* Remove from heat.

Remove the ½ pound butter from the refrigerator to a bowl, and soften it with your fingers. Work quickly so the butter will be soft, cold, but not oily (if it becomes oily, return it to refrigerator to chill).

Using an electric beater, beat the butter you have just softened into the egg-yolk mixture, 2 tablespoons at a time. When all the butter has been beaten in, stop the beater; using a rubber spatula, scrape down the sides of the bowl. Beat in the lemon juice and continue to beat until the mixture forms smooth peaks. With a wooden spoon, mix in the grated lemon rind.

Remove the whipped cream from the refrigerator; using a rubber spatula, fold the whipped cream thoroughly into the buttercream.

Assembling the dacquoise

Invert one of the 9-inch layer-cake pans, and center a dab of the lemon buttercream on it. Set 1 meringue on it evenly (the buttercream will hold the meringue firmly to the pan while you complete the assembly). Using an icing spatula, spread all but 1/4 cup of the buttercream on top of the meringue.

Set the second meringue on the buttercream layer. Spread the remaining 1/4 cup buttercream around the sides of both meringues. Press the sliced almonds against the buttercream on the sides.

Place the *dacquoise*, still on its inverted pan, in the refrigerator to chill for at least 1 hour before serving. Just before serving, sieve 1/4 cup confectioners' sugar on top of the *dacquoise* and with a large metal spatula transfer it to a serving plate.

ORANGE BUTTERCREAM LAYER CAKE

This lavish cake is one example—Lemon Meringue Roll (p. 217) is another—of how traditional textures and flavors can be used as a basis for new variations. Before you take a bird's-eye view of how this cake came about, please note: do not prepare three 9-inch layer-cake pans without first setting them on the middle shelf of your cold oven to be sure the oven space is large enough to hold them. If it is not, prepare two 9-inch layer-cake pans; the ingredient amounts work as well for 2 pans as they do for 3.

Essentially, this layer cake is based on the famous French *génoise,* a batter leavened only with eggs. Culinary history tells us that the *génoise* derived from a more ancient cake which originated in Genoa, Italy. (*Génoise* is French for Genoese.) The batter bakes into a light and airy sponge cake that is probably the most delicate and delicious one ever invented. It is also the most versatile; it accepts all flavors, and finds its way into pans of any size and shape.

Here, the goal was to turn out a layer cake redolent of orange. Grated orange rind was added to the *génoise* batter. When baked and cooled, each layer was saturated with orange-liqueur-flavored syrup. A French buttercream, further heightened with orange, was used to put the layers together, then to frost the cake.

Assembled, it is golden, creamy, and tempting beyond belief! But before being baptized Orange Buttercream Layer Cake, it was allowed to mellow in the refrigerator for 2 hours. Not until then did it finally become what it was meant to be—as sumptuous to taste as it was luxurious to look upon.

(SERVES 8 TO 10)

Prepare three 9-inch layer-cake pans.

2 tablespoons softened butter
2 tablespoons flour

Using some of the softened butter, grease the entire inside of each 9-inch layer-cake pan. Line each pan with wax paper. Do it this way: measure off 3 pieces of wax paper, each one at least 9 inches long. (See p. 190 for illustration of how to fold paper.)

Prepare one lining at a time: Fold the 9-inch piece of wax paper in half. Fold it in half again to form a square. Fold the square in half to form a triangle. Fold the triangle in half to form a pointed cone.

Take hold of the cone, about 1 inch from its tip, between the thumb and index finger of your left hand. Palm up, hold the tip of the cone dead center over the layer-cake pan. Lower the wide end to the rim of the pan. With your right hand, press opened scissors against the inner rim of the pan; using the rim's curve as a guide, cut off the end of the paper cone extending beyond the inner rim.

Open the wax-paper cone: it will be a circle large enough to cover the bottom of the pan.

Fit a paper lining into the bottom of each greased pan, pressing to make it adhere. Using a pastry brush, grease the lining and the sides with the remaining softened butter. Dump 2 teaspoons of the flour into each pan and toss it about to coat the entire bottom and sides. Shake out the excess flour, and set the pans aside.

Preheat oven to 350° F.

CAKES
5 eggs (U.S. Graded Large)
1 cup sugar
1 teaspoon vanilla extract
1 cup all-purpose flour
2 teaspoons grated orange rind
6 tablespoons melted butter, cooled to room
      temperature

Break the eggs into a large bowl. Add the sugar and the vanilla. Beat the ingredients together with an electric mixer until they triple in volume, and the mixture runs off the end of the beater in thick ribbons.

Add ⅓ cup of the flour at a time; sprinkle it over the mixture and, using a rubber spatula, fold it in. Watch carefully for any pockets of dry flour, and fold that flour in. Fold in each third quickly and thoroughly, but with a light touch so as not to decrease the volume of the batter. Scatter the grated orange rind over the batter, and fold it in. Now, 2 tablespoons at a time, fold in the cooled melted butter.

Line up the 3 prepared layer-cake pans, and distribute the batter in them equally, using a rubber spatula to scrape out any batter remaining in the bowl. Smooth the surface of the batter in each pan.

Place the pans on the middle shelf of the oven and bake for 12 to 14 minutes (set your timer), until the surface of the cake is pale gold and the cakes shrink slightly from the sides of the pans.

Remove the cakes from the oven to wire racks, and let them cool in their pans to room temperature.

SYRUP
½ cup cold water
¼ cup sugar
2 tablespoons orange-flavored liqueur (Grand Marnier, Cointreau, Triple-Sec, or Curaçao)

Place the water in a small saucepan and set it over low heat. Stir in the sugar, and let the mixture cook until the sugar has completely dissolved, 4 or 5 minutes.

Set it aside to cool. Keep the liqueur nearby; it will be added later.

ORANGE BUTTERCREAM
3 egg yolks (U.S. Graded Large)
1 cup confectioners' sugar
½ cup hot milk
½ pound (2 sticks) unsalted butter, cold
2 tablespoons orange-flavored liqueur
2 tablespoons grated orange rind

Place the egg yolks in a heavy enamelware saucepan. Add confectioners' sugar all at once; using a wooden spoon, mix the ingredients together until they turn to a smooth paste. Stirring constantly with the wooden spoon, gradually add the hot milk. Continuing to stir, cook the mixture over medium heat until it lightly coats the spoon. *Do not let it come to a boil, or it will curdle.* Remove from the heat.

Pour the contents of the pan into a bowl (use a rubber spatula to remove all of it) and beat it with an electric mixer until it has thickened. Let it stand.

Remove the ½ pound butter from the refrigerator to a bowl and soften it with your fingers. Work quickly so that the butter will be soft, cold, but not oily (if it becomes oily, return it to the refrigerator to chill).

Using an electric beater, beat 2 tablespoons of the softened butter at a time into the mixture. When all the butter has been beaten in, stop the beater; using a rubber spatula, scrape down the sides of the bowl. Add the 2 tablespoons of orange-flavored liqueur. Beat it in, and continue to beat the mixture until it forms smooth peaks. Using a wooden spoon, mix in the 2 tablespoons of grated orange rind. Set the bowl aside.

Assembling the layers

Stir the 2 tablespoons orange-flavored liqueur into the cooled syrup.

Turn the cakes out of their pans, wax-paper side up. Invert one layer-cake pan, put a small dab of buttercream in the middle of it, and set one cake layer on it evenly. (The buttercream will hold the cake firmly to the pan while you complete the assembly.) Peel off the wax paper. Dip a pastry brush into the syrup and brush it on the surface of the cake. Continue to saturate the surface until it has absorbed about one third of the syrup.

Using an icing spatula, evenly spread about 2 tablespoons of buttercream over the entire top of the cake.

Set a second cake layer onto the buttercreamed layer. Peel off the wax paper, and saturate the surface with another third of the syrup. Spread 2 tablespoons of buttercream on the surface. Repeat this procedure with the third cake.

Using an icing spatula, spread 2 tablespoons of buttercream on top smoothly and evenly, then continue all around the sides with as much buttercream as you need to cover the 3 layers.

There should be about ¼ cup buttercream left with which to decorate the cake. Fit a pastry bag with a No. 4 star tube. Fill the bag with the remaining buttercream, and pipe it on top of the cake in any way that pleases you. Place the cake in the refrigerator still on the inverted cake pan, to mellow for at least 2 hours before transferring, with two metal spatulas, to a serving plate.

NOTES:

REFRIGERATOR STORAGE: Safe for 2 to 3 days.

FREEZER STORAGE: Safe for 4 to 6 weeks, if wrapped so as to be airtight. Before serving, defrost overnight in the refrigerator.

The 3 layers of *génoise* can be made into a great strawberry or peach shortcake. Cut the fresh fruit, then lay it out between 2 layers of the *génoise*. Cover the top and sides of the cake with whipped cream sweetened to taste with confectioners' sugar. After covering the top with the whipped cream, decorate it if you like, using the strawberries whole or the fresh peaches sliced.

LEMON MERINGUE ROLL

Génoise, the airy sponge cake that inspired the Orange Butter-cream Layer Cake (p. 212), is also the basis for this Lemon Meringue Roll. Whereas the layer cake is lavish and sumptuous, the roll is exquisite. Although it looks small, it is rich, and serves 8 generously with sometimes a sliver left over. For the intimate dinner party where only the best will do, you can count on having just that with Lemon Meringue Roll.

(SERVES 8)

Prepare a jelly-roll pan

> 4 teaspoons softened butter
> 1 tablespoon flour

With 2 teaspoons of the softened butter, grease a jelly-roll pan 11 × 16 inches. Line the pan with wax paper, leaving an overlap of about 1½ inches at each end to be used later as "handles" when you remove the cake from the pan. With a pastry brush dipped into the remaining 2 teaspoons softened butter, paint a film over the entire surface of the wax paper, leaving the "handles" un-buttered. Scatter the flour over the buttered part of the wax paper. Move the pan about until the flour covers the entire surface, then turn it over and shake off the excess. Set the pan aside.

> *FILLING*
> 3 eggs (U.S. Graded Large)
> ¼ cup granulated sugar
> 2 tablespoons unsalted butter
> ¼ cup fresh lemon juice
> 2 teaspoons grated lemon rind

Preheat oven to 350° F.

Separate the egg yolks from the whites and reserve the whites for the meringue. Drop the egg yolks into a heavy 1-quart enamelware saucepan. Add the sugar, butter, lemon juice and rind. Using a wooden spoon, stir the mixture constantly over medium heat until it thickens; *do not let it come to a boil or it will curdle.* Still stirring, remove from heat and pour the mixture into a bowl. Use a rubber spatula to remove any of the mixture remaining in the saucepan and add it to the bowl. Let the mixture cool to room temperature.

CAKE
3 eggs (U.S. Graded Large)
½ cup sugar
¼ teaspoon vanilla extract
½ cup all-purpose flour, sifted
4 tablespoons melted butter, cooled to room temperature

Break the eggs into a large bowl. Add the sugar and the vanilla. Beat the ingredients together with an electric mixer until they triple in volume and the mixture runs off the end of the beater in thick ribbons.

Add one third of the flour at a time; sprinkle it over the mixture and, using a rubber spatula, fold it in. Watch carefully for any pockets of dry flour, and fold that flour in. Fold each third of flour in quickly and thoroughly, but with a light touch so as not to decrease the volume of the batter.

Now, 2 tablespoons at a time, fold in the cooled melted butter. Still using your rubber spatula, scrape all the batter out of the bowl onto the center of the lined jelly-roll pan, then spread it evenly to cover the whole surface.

Place the pan on the middle shelf of the oven. Bake for 12 to 14 minutes (set your timer), until the surface is pale gold and the cake shrinks slightly from the edges of the pan.

Remove the pan from oven and set it on a wire rack to cool for 10 minutes (set your timer). It should still be slightly warm when you roll it. *Turn oven off.*

Dampen a kitchen towel in cold water, wring it out well, and spread it evenly on your work surface. Lift the cake from the pan by its paper "handles" and set it on the towel so that the long sides of the cake face you. Starting with the edge nearest you, roll up the cake in the paper. Lightly grip paper and cake together, roll them over, and continue rolling them together into a cylinder. Wrap the damp towel around the roll, completely enclosing it, and set aside to cool to room temperature.

Preheat oven to 400° F.

Unwrap the roll, leaving it on the towel. Unroll the cake, leaving it in place on the paper with the long sides facing you. Remove the filling from the refrigerator. Use a rubber spatula to scrape it out of the bowl and onto the center of the cake. With an icing spatula, spread it evenly over the entire surface. Reroll the cake: use the paper again, but this time just as an aid. Starting with the edge nearest you, lightly grip the edges of paper and cake together. Turn them over together, then, as you roll the cake, let the paper come away toward you, separating it from the cake. Continue to roll up the cake, using the paper to turn the cake over, seam side down. Before discarding the paper, stretch it taut over the length of the roll and, cupping your hands, run them over the roll to set it firmly into a cylinder. Discard the paper, and place the cake on an ovenproof serving platter.

MERINGUE
3 egg whites
8 tablespoons granulated sugar
1 tablespoon confectioners' sugar

Beat the egg whites in a bowl with an electric mixer until they froth. Adding 1 tablespoon of the granulated sugar at a time, beat the mixture until it is firm enough to hold its shape on the end of the beater.

Cutting on the diagonal, neatly trim each end of the roll.

Fit a pastry bag with a No. 4 star tube, and spoon all the meringue into the bag. Pipe the meringue onto the top and sides of the cake in ribbonlike rows, one right next to the other, but leave the cut ends of the roll exposed. Transfer the cake, still on its platter, to the middle shelf of the oven. Bake for 7 to 8 minutes (set your timer), until the meringue is very pale brown. Remove the platter from the oven. Sift the confectioners' sugar over the meringue. Serve warm.

NOTES:

If you like a jelly roll, follow the directions exactly as described, but in place of the lemon filling use a jelly or favorite preserve. Before rolling the baked cake, spread the jelly or preserve ¼ inch thick, and proceed with the recipe as described, but do not make the meringue. Before serving, sprinkle the whole top of the roll heavily with confectioners' sugar.

CHOCOLATE SOUR-CREAM LAYER CAKE

The right proportion of chocolate to sour cream and rum brings out their affinity for each other. Used as frosting, it gives the cake a slightly piquant edge.

(SERVES 6 TO 8)

> 2 teaspoons softened butter
> 2 tablespoons flour
> 4 ounces semisweet chocolate
> ¼ pound (1 stick) unsalted butter, softened
> 1¾ cups granulated sugar
> 3 eggs (U.S. Graded Large)
> ½ teaspoon vanilla extract
> 1½ cups all-purpose flour
> Pinch of salt
> 1 teaspoon baking powder
> 1 cup milk

Preheat oven to 375° F.
Prepare two 9-inch layer-cake pans. Using 1 teaspoon of the

softened butter for each one, grease the entire insides of the pans. Dump 1 tablespoon of flour into each pan. Toss it about to coat the entire inside of the pan, then shake out the excess flour. Set the pans aside.

With a large knife, chop the chocolate into small pieces. Melt the chocolate in a small heavy saucepan *over very low heat.* As soon as the chocolate melts, immediately *remove it from heat,* set it aside, and let it cool to room temperature.

With a wooden spoon or an electric mixer, cream ¼ pound butter and the sugar together in a large mixing bowl. One at a time, beat in the eggs until well blended with the mixture. Continuing to beat, add the vanilla, then the cooled chocolate.

Sift the flour, salt, and baking powder together onto a piece of wax paper. First beat about one third of the flour mixture into the chocolate mixture, then one third of the milk. Alternate beating in the flour and milk, one third at a time, until all the ingredients have been incorporated. Continue to beat until the batter is smooth.

Divide the batter evenly into the pans. Place them on the middle shelf of the oven and bake for 20 minutes (set your timer). To test for doneness, insert a wooden toothpick in the middle of one cake. If it comes out clean, both cakes are done. If not, let them bake for 5 minutes more, and test again. Turn the cakes out of the pans and let them cool on wire racks to room temperature.

CHOCOLATE FROSTING
12 ounces semisweet chocolate
1 cup sour cream
Pinch of salt
1 teaspoon vanilla extract
1 tablespoon Cognac or rum

Chop chocolate into small pieces. Melt chocolate in a small heavy saucepan over very low heat. As soon as the chocolate melts, immediately remove it from the heat, and let it cool.

When the chocolate has cooled, beat the sour cream into it. Continuing to beat, add the salt, vanilla, then the Cognac or rum.

Invert 1 layer-cake pan, with a small dab of frosting on it, and set one of the cooled cakes on it evenly. (The frosting will hold the cake firmly to the pan while you complete the assembly.) Using an icing spatula, evenly spread one quarter of the chocolate mixture over the entire top.

Set the second cake on the frosted layer. Frost the top and sides with the remaining chocolate mixture, spreading it smoothly and evenly. Place the cake in the refrigerator still on its inverted pan. Chill for at least 2 hours before transferring it, with 2 metal spatulas, to a serving plate.

NOTES:
REFRIGERATOR STORAGE: Safe for 2 to 3 days.
FREEZER STORAGE: Safe for 4 to 6 weeks if wrapped so as to be airtight. Before serving, defrost overnight in the refrigerator.

FROZEN CHOCOLATE-COFFEE TORTE

If you have time, it's worth making this dessert when you don't need it. It keeps safely in the freezer for up to 3 weeks—so it's like having a glorious dessert in the bank. What better way to be prepared for a spontaneous party? Transfer it from the freezer to the refrigerator an hour before you plan to serve it.

Make sure the middle shelf of your oven can hold three 9-inch layer-cake pans.

(SERVES 8 TO 10)

2 tablespoons softened butter
2 tablespoons flour

CAKE LAYERS
6 ounces semisweet chocolate, cut into small pieces
5 eggs (U.S. Graded Large), separated
½ cup granulated sugar
1 teaspoon vanilla extract
½ cup confectioners' sugar

COFFEE CREAM
4 teaspoons instant espresso coffee
2 teaspoons hot water
1½ cups heavy cream, chilled
3 tablespoons confectioners' sugar, sifted

Preheat oven to 350° F.
Prepare three 9-inch layer-cake pans exactly as described on pages 212 and 213, and set them aside.

CAKE LAYERS

Melt the chocolate pieces in a 1-quart heavy saucepan over *very low heat.* As soon as the chocolate is melted, remove the pan from heat, set it aside, and let it cool to room temperature.

In a large bowl, beat the egg whites with an electric mixer until they hold soft peaks. Gradually adding the granulated sugar, continue to beat until the whites hold stiff peaks.

In a small bowl, beat the egg yolks together until they are well combined.

Beat the combined yolks into the cooled chocolate. Beat in the vanilla. Using a rubber spatula, fold one third of the beaten egg whites thoroughly into the chocolate mixture.

Pour this mixture into the remaining egg whites; still using the rubber spatula, fold them together. Fold quickly and thoroughly but with a light touch so as not to decrease the volume of the egg whites.

Line up the 3 prepared layer-cake pans. Using the rubber spatula, divide the mixture equally into the pans. Scrape out any remaining in the bowl, add it, then smooth the surface of the mixture in each pan.

Place the pans on the middle shelf of the oven and bake for 12 minutes (set your timer). Test for doneness by inserting a wooden toothpick into one of the layers. If it comes out clean, all the layers are done. If it does not, let them bake for 2 minutes more, and test again.

While the layers bake, tear off a sheet of wax paper at least 27 inches long, or 3 sheets each 9 inches long. Smooth the wax paper on the work surface and sift over its entire surface the ½ cup confectioners' sugar.

Remove the pans from the oven. Turn out each layer, top side down, onto the sugared paper. (The sugar will prevent the layers from sticking while they cool.) Peel off and discard the pan linings and let the layers cool to room temperature. While the layers cool, prepare the Coffee Cream.

COFFEE CREAM

Dissolve the coffee in the water. In a large mixing bowl, beat the chilled cream with an electric mixer until it holds soft peaks. Continuing to beat, add the coffee, then, 1 tablespoon at a time, the confectioners' sugar.

Assembling the torte

Invert one of the layer-cake pans and center a dab of the whipped cream on it (the cream will hold the cake layer firmly to the pan while you complete the assembly). Set one cake layer evenly on the pan and, using an icing spatula, evenly spread about ½ cup of the coffee cream on the top. Repeat this procedure with the second layer, then with the third, spreading the remaining coffee cream on the top and all around the sides.

Place the torte, still on the inverted pan, in the freezer. Let it chill, uncovered, until it becomes firm. Cover with plastic wrap, and return to the freezer. At 1 hour before serving, unwrap the torte, and store it in the refrigerator; it should be very firm when served. Transfer the torte with 2 metal spatulas from the inverted pan to a serving plate.

SAVARIN CHANTILLY

Savarin Chantilly will be enjoyed by those who prefer a dessert that is not too sweet. It is a *baba au rhum* baked in a ring mold. Turned out of the mold, the center is then filled with vanilla-flavored whipped cream—the *chantilly*. Fresh fruits such as strawberries, raspberries, or sliced fresh peaches may be folded into the *chantilly* as a filling for the center. Or the fruits may fill the center with the *chantilly* served separately in a bowl.

(SERVES 6)

> 1 tablespoon unsalted butter softened (for greasing ring mold)
> 1 package (¼ ounce) active dry yeast
> ¼ cup warm water (110° to 115° F.)
> 3 tablespoons sugar
> 1½ cups all-purpose flour
> 3 eggs (U.S. Graded Large)
> ¼ cup milk
> 6 tablespoons unsalted butter, softened

With the 1 tablespoon softened butter, grease the whole inside of a 4-cup ring mold and set it aside.

CAKE

Add the yeast to the warm water, then ½ teaspoon of the sugar; using a fork, stir the ingredients together a few times. With your finger, wipe down into the mixture any yeast granules clinging to the fork. Set the mixture aside; the yeast will soon begin to foam and increase in volume.

Place the flour in a large mixing bowl. Add the eggs, milk, remaining sugar, and the yeast mixture; using a wooden spoon, beat the ingredients together until they turn to a smooth batter. Cover the bowl with a towel, and let the batter rise for 45 minutes (set your timer), or until doubled in volume.   **1st rise**

Using a wooden spoon, stir down the batter. One tablespoon at a time, beat in the 6 tablespoons softened butter, and continue to beat until you see only small specks of it in the batter. Scrape the batter into the ring mold, cover with a towel, and let it rise for 35 minutes (set your timer), or until it comes to about ½ inch below the top of the mold.   **2nd rise**

Preheat oven to 375° F.

When the batter has risen sufficiently, place the ring mold on the middle shelf of the oven and bake for 10 minutes (set your timer). Immediately, reduce heat to 350° F. and continue to bake the cake for 15 minutes (set your timer), or until the top is golden brown. Remove the ring mold from the oven, and turn the cake out onto a cake rack to cool to room temperature.

While the cake cools, make the syrup.

SYRUP
1 cup water
½ cup sugar
¼ cup dark rum

Pour the water into a small saucepan and set it over low heat. Stir in the sugar, and let the mixture cook until the sugar completely dissolves, 4 or 5 minutes. Set it aside to cool. Keep the rum nearby; it will be added later.

When the cake has cooled to room temperature, set it on a serving dish. Stir the rum into the cooled syrup, and slowly spoon the syrup onto the top of the cake, adding more syrup as the cake fully absorbs it. Continue spooning it on until the cake has absorbed all of the syrup. Set the cake aside and make the filling.

CREAM CHANTILLY
1 cup heavy cream
1 teaspoon vanilla extract
2 tablespoons confectioners' sugar

Whip the cream until it holds soft peaks. Stir in the vanilla, then the sugar. Spoon the whipped cream into the center of the cake ring and serve at once.

BLUEBERRY DUMPLING PIE

Varied only a little, Blueberry Dumpling Pie is the traditional French Canadian *Cipâte aux Bleuets*—three-crust blueberry pie. The filling for the traditional pie contains blueberries, sugar, and lemon juice. This variation includes red-currant jelly as well, which gives it a slightly different flavor while reducing the amount of sugar usually used.

Although the dessert is known as a three-crusted pie, the middle layer of pastry is never exposed to the dry heat of the oven. It steams in the blueberry juice, absorbs some of its flavor, and cooks just like a dumpling. You'll be surprised by the beautiful contrasts: crisp top crust, luscious berries, and flavorous dumpling.

(SERVES 8 TO 10)

FILLING
6 cups fresh blueberries
½ cup red-currant jelly
1 cup sugar
2 tablespoons tapioca
4 teaspoons fresh lemon juice
2 teaspoons sugar
¼ teaspoon ground cinnamon

PASTRY
1½ recipes Flaky Pastry (p. 25)

GLAZE
1 egg
2 tablespoons cream or milk

Dump the berries into a colander, then wash them under cold running water. Sifting through them with your fingers, remove and discard all stems, and any unripe or bruised berries. Shake the colander so the berries roll about and excess water drains off. Transfer the berries to a bowl, and set them aside.

Melt the currant jelly in a small saucepan over low heat. Thoroughly combine 1 cup sugar and the tapioca, then sprinkle the mixture over the berries. Pour the melted jelly over. Use a rubber spatula to remove any jelly remaining in the saucepan and add it to the bowl. Add the lemon juice. Using the rubber spatula, lightly toss the berry mixture until all the ingredients are well distributed. Set the bowl aside.

PASTRY

Preheat oven to 400° F.

Remove the pastry from the refrigerator, unwrap, and place it on a lightly floured surface. Elongate the rounded pastry by pressing it with the flat of your hand, then shape it into a rectangle. With a sharp knife, divide it into 3 equal pieces. One at a time, shape each piece into a ball. With the flat of your hand, press each ball of pastry into a thick cake, then shape the sides into a round. Loosely wrap 2 pastry rounds in separate pieces of wax paper, and return them to the refrigerator.

Lightly flour the top of the remaining piece of pastry and your rolling pin. Roll the pastry into a circular shape, always rolling out from the center and ending each stroke just short of the edge so as not to thin out the edge too soon; you need a little thickness to hold when you turn it. Never roll back toward the center. Turn the pastry clockwise from time to time to test if it is sticking. If it sticks, flour lightly underneath. Continue rolling out the pastry until it is about 12 inches in diameter.

Set a 9-inch pie pan alongside the rolled-out pastry. Place the rolling pin on the part of the pastry which is farthest from you. With the aid of a metal spatula, lift the far edge of the pastry onto the back of the rolling pin. Using your fingertips, lightly press the pastry against the back of the rolling pin—just enough to make it adhere—and roll the pastry toward yourself, *making 1 complete turn.*

Lift the pastry-covered rolling pin by the handles, allowing the pastry to hang down freely. Suspending the free pastry above the pie pan, bring it forward to the edge of the pan nearest you. Let 1 inch of the pastry drop over the front edge. Now, unrolling away from yourself, let the pastry fall slackly into the pan.

Spoon two thirds of the blueberry mixture into the pastry-lined pan, spread it evenly over the bottom, and set the pan aside.

Remove one of the reserved pieces of pastry from the refrigerator. Again, lightly flour your work surface. Unwrap, and place the pastry on it. Repeat the procedure of rolling it out as just described, but this time to a circle 9 inches in diameter. Invert a 9-inch plate on the pastry. Using the rim of the plate as a guide, trim the edge of the pastry with a small sharp knife. Gently lift the circle of pastry and place it so it lies smoothly on top of the blueberry-mixture in the pie pan.

Spoon the remaining berry mixture onto the 9-inch pastry circle. Spread it evenly, then set the pan aside.

Remove the remaining piece of pastry from the refrigerator, repeat the procedure of rolling it out, and this time to a circle 10 inches in diameter. Dip your index finger into cold water, then dampen the pastry covering the rim of the pan.

Lift the circle of pastry onto the rolling pin just as described for lining the pan. Suspending the free pastry above the pan, bring it forward to the edge of the pan nearest you. Now, unrolling away from yourself, let the pastry fall slackly over the pie.

Using scissors, trim the excess pastry from around the rim of the pan, or, holding a sharp knife at an angle, slash it away. With your finger, test the pastry on the rim of the pan for dampness. If it is not damp, dip your finger into cold water and dampen it again. With your fingertips, press the top and bottom edges of the pastry together. To seal the 2 edges more firmly, press them together with the back of fork tines.

Cut a vent in the center of the top crust: with a small sharp knife or 1-inch round cookie cutter, cut out a circle of pastry about 1 inch in diameter.

Beat the egg and cream (or milk) together until well combined. Using a pastry brush, paint a film of the mixture over the entire surface of the pastry. Mix 2 teaspoons sugar and the cinnamon together well, and sprinkle the mixture on the glaze.

Set the pie on the middle shelf of the oven and bake for 30

minutes (set your timer). *Reduce heat to 350° F.*, and let the pie bake for 30 minutes more (set your timer), or until the top is golden brown. Serve warm.

NOTE:
If you live in an area where huckleberries are available, they may be substituted for the blueberries.

UPSIDE-DOWN APPLE PIE

This recipe harks back to the traditional French *Tarte Tatin*, an upside-down apple tart. Turned out of the pan it bakes in, a perfect-tasting and superbly attractive *Tarte Tatin* consists of evenly caramelized layers of apples resting on a very thin crust. Recipes for *Tarte Tatin* read convincingly, but complete and uniform caramelization depends on the juiciness of the apples— too much or too little juice produces disappointing results.

Upside-Down Apple Pie, although strongly reminiscent of the original, is quite a different dish. The puff pastry bakes into a high, delicate, flaky base for the apples to rest on. The apricot preserve, while it adds a distinctive flavor that *Tarte Tatin* doesn't have, also insures a predictably smooth and attractive topping that camouflages imperfect caramelization.

(SERVES 6 TO 8)

> 6 tablespoons unsalted butter
> ¾ cup granulated sugar
> 3 pounds MacIntosh apples
> ⅓ recipe Puff Pastry (p. 30)
> ⅓ cup apricot preserve

With 4 tablespoons of the unsalted butter, coat the bottom and sides of a 10-inch iron skillet. Sprinkle the buttered bottom and sides with ½ cup of the sugar.

Peel and core the apples, then cut them into slices ¼ inch thick. Arrange the apple slices in the pan in layers, mounding them slightly at the center, leaving about ¼ inch of the inside rim of the pan exposed. Dot each layer with bits of the remaining butter. Top each buttered layer with a sprinkle of the remaining sugar. Set the skillet aside.

PUFF PASTRY

Remove the chilled pastry from the refrigerator, unwrap, and place it on a lightly floured surface. Dust the top of the pastry lightly with flour, and roll it out into an 11- or 12-inch square, approximately ¼ inch thick. Set an inverted 10-inch dinner plate on it as a guide and, with a small sharp knife, cut out a 10-inch disc. Lay the disc loosely on the mounded apples, letting the edge of the pastry touch the exposed inner rim of the skillet.

With a sharp knife, cut a vent at top center into the pastry, then place the skillet in the refrigerator and let pastry chill for 20 minutes.

Preheat oven to 425° F., and set a cookie sheet on the middle shelf of the oven.

Remove the skillet from the refrigerator, and place it on the cookie sheet in the oven. *Reduce oven heat to 350° F.*, and bake the pie for 40 minutes (set your timer), or until the pastry is deep gold.

Remove the skillet from oven. If you can see the butter-sugar mixture bubbling around the edge of the pastry, set the skillet over medium heat and let the juices cook away until the mixture is no longer bubbling. Let the pie set at room temperature for 30 minutes.

Place an inverted cake plate over the top of the skillet. With both hands, hold plate and skillet together tightly, then turn them over. Lift the skillet.

Spoon the apricot preserve into a small saucepan, and melt it over low heat. Push it through a fine sieve onto the surface of the apples, spreading it evenly with a metal spatula. Serve warm immediately, or at room temperature. If you like, serve Upside-Down Apple Pie with whipped cream.

NOTE:
Although it will not rise as high, Pseudo Puff Pastry (p. 39) may be substituted for Puff Pastry. Or you may use Cream Cheese Pastry (p. 24), which will not rise at all but lends a complementary flavor to the apples.

ONE-CRUST RHUBARB PIE

Rhubarb, the shrublike perennial, is the announcer of spring. And spring is a good time to make this lovely-looking and delicious pie. In supermarkets and most vegetable stores, the rhubarb we see is shorn of its big, tough leaves. New gardeners and shoppers from roadside stands often end up with huge bunches, leaves and all. Someone who didn't know better, but should have, adventurously cooked the leaves and ate them. The person lived—but to regret it for a while; the leaves are poisonous, and should be cut off and discarded.

One-Crust Rhubarb Pie is especially pretty to look at because of its color. Cooked, it turns pale pink, but the addition of raspberry preserve intensifies the color, bringing it back to the bright pink of the raw stems. The flavor of raspberries complements that of rhubarb, and the sweetness of the preserve makes it possible to reduce the amount of sugar usually called for to cut the tartness. Be sure to bake your pie in a glass pie dish as instructed in the recipe. Baked in a metal pan, the rhubarb takes on a metallic taste.

(SERVES 8)

FILLING
2 pounds fresh rhubarb, leaves cut off and root ends
    trimmed
1½ cups granulated sugar
¼ cup quick-cooking tapioca
1 teaspoon freshly grated lemon rind
3 tablespoons unsalted butter
½ cup raspberry preserve

PASTRY
1 recipe Cream Cheese Pastry (p. 24)

GLAZE
1 egg yolk
2 tablespoons cream or milk
1½ teaspoons granulated sugar

Preheat oven to 400° F.

Wash the rhubarb stalks under cold running water, then pat
them dry with paper towels. Cut them into ½-inch-thick chunks
and put them into a large mixing bowl.

In a small mixing bowl, combine the sugar, tapioca, and lemon
rind, tossing together until well blended.

Over medium heat, melt the butter in a small heavy saucepan,
then stir in the raspberry preserve. When the preserve has melted,
turn off heat.

Strain the preserve through a fine-meshed sieve into a small
bowl, pressing down hard to extract the seeds. Discard the seeds.

Assembling the filling

Sprinkle the sugar, tapioca, lemon-rind mixture over the rhubarb chunks. Using a wooden spoon, combine the ingredients
until all the rhubarb is coated with the sugar mixture. Add the
raspberry preserve and mix it thoroughly with the coated rhubarb.
Scrape the contents of the bowl into a 10-inch ovenproof glass pie
dish, and set aside.

PASTRY

Remove the pastry from the refrigerator, unwrap, and place it on a lightly floured surface. Lightly flour the top of the pastry and your rolling pin.

Roll out the pastry into a circular shape, always rolling out from the center and ending each stroke just short of the edge so as not to thin out the edge too soon; you need a little thickness to hold when you turn it. Never roll back toward the center. Turn the pastry clockwise from time to time to test if it is sticking to the surface. If it sticks, flour lightly underneath. Continue rolling the pastry out until it is about 12 inches in diameter and ⅛ inch thick.

Set the pie dish alongside the rolled-out pastry. Place the rolling pin on the part of the pastry which is farthest from you. With the aid of a metal spatula, lift the far edge of the pastry onto the back of the rolling pin. Using your fingertips, lightly press the pastry against the back of the rolling pin—just enough to make it adhere—and roll the pastry toward yourself, making *1 complete turn*.

Lift the pastry-covered rolling pin by the handles, allowing the pastry to hang down freely. Suspending the free pastry above the dish, bring it forward to the edge of the dish nearest you. Let 1 inch of the pastry drop over the front edge. Now, unrolling away from yourself, let the pastry fall slackly over the filled dish. Keep

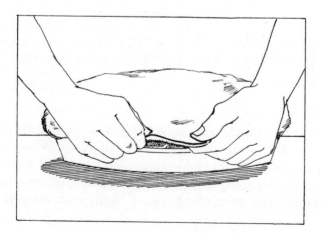

the pin *above* the edge when unrolling; the weight of the pin on the edge can cut the pastry.

With scissors, neatly trim the edge of the 1 inch of overhanging pastry. A little at a time, first turn it under to double its thickness, then set it back on the rim of the dish so as to lie flush with the edge.

Flute the edge of the pastry. Visualize the dish as the face of a clock. Lightly press thumb and index finger of your left hand on the pastry rim at 3 o'clock. Lightly press the index finger of the

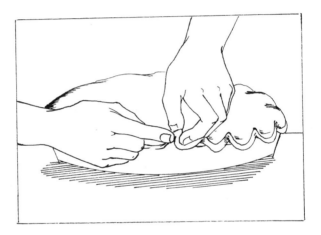

other hand *between,* and gently push the pastry a fraction toward the filling. *Staying at 3 o'clock* and turning the dish counterclockwise, continue making these scallops all around the rim.

GLAZE

Beat the egg yolk and cream or milk together until well combined. Using a pastry brush, paint a film of the mixture on the entire surface of the pastry. Sprinkle the 1½ teaspoons of sugar on the glaze. Set a jelly-roll pan on the middle shelf of the oven, then place the pie dish on it, and bake for 15 minutes (set your timer).

Reduce heat to 350° F., and bake for 30 to 40 minutes (set your timer), or until the crust is deep brown. Remove the dish and set it on a cake rack to cool.

Serve the pie warm or at room temperature. Either way, it is especially good served with a little heavy cream.

APRICOT TURNOVERS

These crisp airy turnovers are equally enjoyable as a dinner dessert or for breakfast. They are no sweeter than Danish pastries.

(MAKES 9 TURNOVERS)

> ⅓ portion Puff Pastry (p. 30)
> ½ cup apricot preserve
> ½ cup confectioners' sugar

Remove the puff pastry from the refrigerator, unwrap, and place it horizontally on a lightly floured work surface. Carefully measure and cut off one third of it, then rewrap and freeze (or refreeze) the remainder.

Lightly flour the surface of the pastry and your rolling pin, and roll the pastry into a square. Evenly distributing your weight on the handles of the rolling pin, roll it on the pastry all the way to the edges—first away from yourself, then back toward yourself. To test for sticking, run a metal spatula underneath the pastry. If it sticks, dust underneath lightly with flour. Continue rolling until the square measures approximately 13 inches.

With a sharp knife or a pastry wheel and a ruler as a guide, trim the edges of the pastry into an exact 12-inch square.

Measure and mark the pastry into thirds, first horizontally, then vertically. Using the ruler as a guide, cut the pastry—gridiron fashion—into nine 4-inch squares. Separate the squares; with a pastry brush dipped lightly into water, dampen the edges. Using slightly under 1 tablespoon of the apricot preserve for each square, center a mound on each one.

One at a time, lift a corner of each square and fold it over the filling to form a triangle. With your fingertips, gently press the dampened edges together, sealing in the preserve.

Run cold water over a large cookie sheet, shake off the excess, and line up the turnovers on it about 1 inch apart. With the tip of a small sharp knife, make 3 small slits at top center of each turnover. Place the cookie sheet in the refrigerator for 20 minutes (set your timer), and *preheat oven to 450° F.*

Transfer the cookie sheet from the refrigerator to the middle shelf of the oven and bake for 10 minutes (set your timer). *Reduce heat to 400° F.*, and bake for 10 minutes more (set your timer), or until the turnovers are golden brown.

Remove the cookie sheet from oven. *Raise heat to 500° F.* Using a small sieve, sprinkle the top of each turnover heavily with confectioners' sugar, return them to the middle shelf of the oven, and bake for 3 or 4 minutes more, or until the sugar has melted.

Remove the cookie sheet from oven. With the aid of a metal spatula, slide the turnovers—top side up—onto a wire rack. Cool to room temperature.

NOTE:
If you prefer the filling more tart, add ½ to 1 teaspoon grated lemon rind to the preserve. Stir it in a little at a time, determining the degree of tartness according to your taste.

BAKED PEARS

Any type of pear may be used in making this recipe, but none has the graceful contour of the bell-shaped Bosc. As dessert for a luncheon or dinner party, Bosc pears lend a touch of elegance. Whichever type of pear you choose, Baked Pears in their sauce keep well in the refrigerator for as long as 5 days.

(SERVES 6)

> 4 cups cold water
> 2 lemons
> 6 Bosc pears, approximately the same size and ripeness, with their stems
> 1½ cups sugar
> 2½ cups cold water
> ¼ cup Grand Marnier liqueur
> Approximately 2 tablespoons grated lemon rind

Preheat oven to 375° F.

Put the 4 cups of cold water in a large bowl. Cut the lemons into halves and squeeze their juice into the water. When its juice is extracted, add the lemon rind to the water. Use a vegetable peeler to peel each pear, leaving the stem intact. As each pear is peeled, place it in the lemon water. (The acidulated water prevents discoloration of the pears.)

Put the sugar in a 3- to 4-inch-deep ovenproof casserole large enough to hold the pears in one layer. Pour the 2½ cups of cold water over the sugar, stirring it in. Lifting each pear by its stem, lay the pears on their sides in the casserole. Cover the casserole tightly with aluminum foil, and place it on the lower middle shelf of the oven. Bake for 20 minutes (set your timer).

To test for doneness, insert the tip of a sharp knife into the fleshiest part of one pear. If it is resistant, cover the dish and bake for about 5 minutes more, or until the pears are tender.

Remove the casserole from oven and cool the pears to room temperature. Stir the Grand Marnier, then the grated lemon rind, into the sauce. Chill the pears in their sauce for at least 2 hours. When serving, ladle the sauce generously over each pear.

CARAMEL CUSTARD TART

Traditionally, a *crème caramel* is custard cooked in a vessel that has been lined with caramel. Unmolded, the custard is topped with the caramel, which then becomes its sauce. What gives Caramel Custard Tart its unusual flavor is beating the caramel into the custard before baking it in the tart shell, and the pastry is delicious on its own. The fluted shell makes a beautiful container, and its flakiness adds textural contrast to the smoothness of the filling.

(SERVES 6)

> 1 cup milk
> 1 cup heavy cream
> ½ cup granulated sugar
> 4 egg yolks (U.S. Graded Large)
> 2 teaspoons Port wine
> 1 Prebaked Tart Shell (p. 27)

In a small saucepan, stir the milk and cream together until well combined, then cook over medium heat until bubbles form around the edge. Turn the heat to simmer, or to low, to keep the mixture warm.

Sprinkle the sugar into an 8- to 10-inch heavy skillet. Stirring constantly with a wooden spoon, cook the sugar over medium heat until it melts, then caramelizes—turning light amber, or tea-colored.

Turn the heat to simmer; still stirring constantly with the spoon, add the cream mixture, pouring it gradually into the caramel, $\frac{1}{4}$ cup at a time. Let the mixture cook until the caramel dissolves completely. (After adding the cream mixture, the caramel may lump up on the spoon; leave the spoon in the mixture until the caramel dissolves completely.)

While the mixture cooks, separate the eggs (store the whites for another use), and beat the yolks together with a wire whisk until they are well blended. Gradually whisk the caramel-cream mixture into the beaten yolks. Stir in the Port wine. Allow the mixture to cool to room temperature.

Preheat oven to 375° F.

Set the prebaked tart shell in its tin on a surface conveniently close to the oven. Pour the cooled caramel mixture into the shell and place it on the lower middle shelf of the oven. Bake for 30 minutes (set your timer), or until the caramel custard has set.

Test for doneness by inserting the tip of a knife into the center of the custard. If the knife comes out clean, the custard has set. Remove the tin from the oven to a wire rack and cool the tart to room temperature. Place it in the refrigerator to chill in its tin for 2 hours before serving.

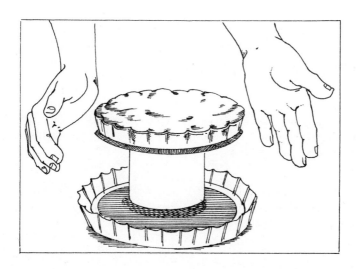

To remove the tart from the tin

Set a tall coffee can (or any other container resembling it in height and shape) on your work surface. Have your cake dish nearby. Set the tart in its tin on top of the can. (See p. 241 for illustration of this instruction.) Gently loosen the metal outer rim from the baked tart shell and bring it down to the work surface. Transfer the tart from the top of the can to the serving dish. The tart will still be attached to the metal bottom of the tart tin. If you prefer to remove the metal bottom, ease the tart off onto the dish with the aid of a metal spatula.

NOTE:
If you've never made pastry before, or never lined a tart tin with pastry, make Caramel Custard Tart with Cream Cheese Pastry (p. 24) the first time; it's extremely easy to handle.

Converting to the Metric System

The figures in the little tables in the text have been rounded off to the nearest whole number or convenient fraction. A more accurate figure may be printed in these tables, but you can work out an even more accurate figure by making the conversion yourself.

Temperature   F. = Fahrenheit   C. = Celsius (Centigrade)

Conversion factor, Fahrenheit to Celsius: subtract 32 from the Fahrenheit figure; multiply the result by 5, then divide that figure by 9.
Conversion factor, Celsius to Fahrenheit: multiply Celsius figure by 9, divide by 5, and add 32.

° Fahrenheit	° Celsius	
32	0	(water freezes)
110	43.3	
115	46.1	

° Fahrenheit	° Celsius	
170	76.7	
212	100	(water boils)
325	163	
350	177	
370	187.7	
375	190.5	
400	204.4	
425	218.3	
450	232	
500	260	

OUNCES AND POUNDS

Conversion factor, ounces to grams: multiply ounce figure by 28.3 to get number of grams. 1 gram × 1000 = 1 kilogram. Conversion factor, grams to ounces: multiply gram figure by .0353 to get number of ounces.

Ounces	Grams
¼	7
1	28.3
3	84.8
4	113.2
6	169.8
8 (½ pound)	226.4
10	283
¼ pound	113.2
½ pound	226.4
1 pound	453.6 = 0.4536 kilogram

Conversion factor, pounds into grams: multiply pound figure by 453.59 to get number of grams.

INCHES

Conversion factor, inches to centimeters: multiply inch figure by 2.54 to get number of centimeters.
Conversion factor, centimeters to inches: multiply centimeter figure by .39 to get number of inches.

Inches	Centimeters
¹⁄₁₆	.159
⅛	.318
¼	.636
½	1.27
1	2.54
1½	3.81
2	5.08
10	25.4
15	38.1

1 centimeter = 10 millimeters.
1 meter = 100 centimeters = 1000 millimeters.

LIQUID VOLUME MEASURES

Liquids include water, milk, wine, and also such apparent solids as butter and sugar, both of which count as liquids in baking. The volume measures will be filled exactly, to the brim for spoon measures, to the marked levels for cups. The teaspoon measure equals ⅓ tablespoon; the tablespoon measure equals ½ ounce; the cup measure equals 8 ounces; the quart measure equals 2 pounds. For quick conversion 1 liter can be substituted for 1 quart.

Teaspoons	Grams
¼	1.17
½	2.34
1	4.7
2	9.4
3 (1 tablespoon)	14.3

Tablespoons	Grams
1	14.3
2 (1 ounce)	28.3
3	42.4
4 (¼ cup)	56.7
6	84.8
8 (½ cup)	114

Liters	Cups
¼	.059
⅓	.079
½	.118 (118.2 cubic centimeters)
⅔	.158
¾	.177
1	.236
1½	.354
2	.473
4 (1 quart)	.946
5	1.18
8 (2 quarts)	1.89
10 quarts	9.46

DRY VOLUME MEASURES

It is impossible to give more than an approximate figure for these, as the weight for the volume unit depends on the ingredient being weighed. The figures in the small table are based on the weight of all-purpose flour, with the volume measure filled level. However, flour is different from bag to bag, and the amount of liquid in the grain makes even this measure inexact.

Complete tables for fractions and multiples can be found in *Units of Weight and Measure*, National Bureau of Standards, U.S. Department of Commerce, Miscellaneous Publication 286, Washington, D.C.

Index

Barbecue sauce, roast fresh ham
  with, 166–167
Barley
  casserole, 197
  -mushroom soup, 93
Bass, striped
  Eleanor, 122–123
  stuffed, 119–121
Beans, dried, black bean soup,
  89–90
Beard, James, 1, 2, 208
Beef
  braised fresh brisket of, 156–157
  broth, 83–84
    canned, 151, 153
  Coney Island cocktail turnovers,
    68–69
  Flemish stew, 152–153
  leftovers, 84n, 157n
  roast filet of, on puff pastry
    rounds, 149–151
  sauerbraten, 154–156
  in stuffed cabbage, 171–173
  tongue, braised, 158–159
Black bean soup, 89–90
Blue cheese cocktail turnovers, 70
Blueberry dumpling pie, 228–231
Bread, 97–115
  caraway rye, 109–111
  cheese, 112–114
  French, mock, 106–108
  Irish soda, 115
  white, 99–102
  whole wheat, 103–105
Bread crumbs, fresh, 76n, 126n,
  141n, 163n, 165n, 178n
Broccoli mold, 184–185
Broth
  beef, 83–84
    canned, 151, 153

chicken
  canned, 151, 153
  golden, 81–82
Buck, Dr. Paul, 4–5
Butter for pastry, 22
Buttercream orange layer cake,
  212–216

C

Cabbage
  leftovers, 183
  red, 183
  stuffed, 171–173
Cakes
  almond, 201–205
  cheesecake, 205–207
  chocolate sour-cream layer, 220–
    222
  génoise, 212, 216, 217
  jelly rolls, 220
  lemon dacquoise, 208–211
  lemon meringue roll, 217–220
  orange buttercream layer, 212–
    216
  shortcake, strawberry or peach,
    216
Caramel custard tart, 240–242
Caraway rye bread, 109–111
Carrots and onions, braised, 180
Casseroles, 10
  barley, 197
  potato cheese, 195
Cheese
  blue cheese cocktail turnovers,
    70
  bread, 112–114
  crabmeat ramekins with, 56–57

Green pepper and onion pizza
    ramekins, 59
Green split pea soup, 91–92

H

Haddock Méditerranée, 124–125
Ham
    baked in a pastry cape, 168–170
    leftovers, 167n, 170n
    roast fresh, with barbecue sauce,
      166–167
Ham bone for soup, 170n
Herbed cocktail wafers, 50–51
Hibben, Sheila, 208
Hors d'oeuvres, *see* Appetizers
Huckleberry dumpling pie, 231n

I

Inches, conversion factor, 245
Irish soda bread, 115
Italian style clams or mussels,
    baked, 77–78

J

Jelly rolls, 220n

L

Lamb, shoulder chops Middle
    Eastern style, 164

Leek(s)
    braised, 181
    and potato soup, 85–87
    preparing, 85–87
Leftovers
    beef, 84n, 157n
    cabbage, 183n
    chicken, 131n, 141n
    ham, 167n, 170n
Lemon
    dacquoise, 208–211
    meringue roll, 217–220
Lentil soup, 88
Liquid volume measures, 245–246
Luncheon menus, 15–16

M

Madeira sauce for roast filet of
    beef, 149–151
*Mastering the Art of French
    Cooking*
    (Beck, Bertholle, and Child), 3
Matzoh balls, 81
Measuring utensils, 9
Menus, 13–17
    cocktail party, 17
    dinner party, 14–15
    luncheon, 15–16
    picnic, 16
Meringue
    for lemon *dacquoise*, 209, 210
    lemon roll, 217–220
Metric system, converting to, 243–
    247
    dry volume measures, 247
    inches, 245
    liquid volume measures, 245–246

Metric system (*continued*)
  ounces, 244
  pounds, 244
  temperature, 243–244
Middle Eastern style lamb chops,
    164
Mixing bowls, 10
Mushroom
  -barley soup, 93
  -onion cocktail turnovers, 67
  pizza ramekins, 59–61
Mussels, baked Italian style, 77–78
Mustard glaze, roast pork with, 165

N

New York Times Magazine, 208
New Yorker, The, 208

O

Onion(s)
  and carrots, braised, 180
  and green pepper pizza rame-
    kins, 59
  -mushroom cocktail turnovers,
    67
Orange buttercream layer cake,
    212–216
Ounces, conversion factor, 244
Oysters, baked, 76

P

Pastry
  for almond cake, 202–204

for blueberry dumpling pie,
    228–230
for chicken pie, 128, 130–131
for cocktail turnovers, 64–65
cream cheese, 24
  for apple pie, upside-down,
    233n
  for caramel custard tart, 242n
flaky, 25–26
ham baked in a cape of, 168–170
for herbed cocktail wafers, 50–51
ingredients for, 22–23
  butter, 22
  flour, 22
  vegetable shortening, 22–23
lining a tart tin with, 28–29
puff, 30–43
  for apple pie, upside-down,
    232
  for apricot turnovers, 237–238
  basic recipe, 30–34
  beef filet on, 149–151
  chicken on, 131n
  fleurons, 36–37, 136
  pseudo, 39–43
  pseudo, for apple pie, upside-
    down, 233n
  rounds, 37–38, 131n, 149–151
  scraps, 36–38
for rhubarb pie, one-crust, 234–
    236
sausage in, 62–63
for savory sticks, 47–49
for savory turnovers, 26n
tart shell
  fillet of sole in, 73–75
  prebaked, 27–29
Pastry sticks, savory, 47–49
Pâté, country, 71–72
Peach shortcake, 216n

S

Salad
  egg, 105n
  tossed green, 13
Sauce
  barbecue, roast fresh ham with, 166–167
  for chicken pie, 128, 129, 131n
  for crabmeat au gratin rame- kins, 56–57
  cranberry, for roast ducks, 142– 145
  for curried shrimp ramekins, 54–55
  Dugléré, 73–75
  for fillet of sole in tart shell, 73– 75
  Madeira, for roast filet of beef, 149–151
  red-wine, chicken in, 136–138
  soubise, 193–194
  sour cream, pheasant with, 146– 148
  for stuffed cabbage, 172–173
  tomato, for pizza ramekins, 58
  white-wine, chicken in, 134–135
Saucepans, 10
Sauerbraten, 154–156
Sausage
  in pastry, 62–63
  pizza ramekins, 59
Sauté pans, 10
Savarin chantilly, 226–227
Savory pastry sticks, 47–49
Savory turnovers, pastry for, 26n
Scallops, baked, 126
Shellfish
  baked, 76

clams, baked, 76
  Italian style, 77–78
crabmeat au gratin ramekins, 56–57
curried shrimp for toast rame- kins, 54–55
mussels baked Italian style, 77– 78
oysters, baked, 76
scallops, baked, 126
Shortcake, strawberry or peach, 216n
Shrimp, curried, for toast rame- kins, 54–55
Skillets, 10
Soda bread, Irish, 115
Sole, fillet of, in a tart shell, 73–75
Soubise sauce, 193–194
Soufflé, spinach, 187–188
Soup, 79–95
  beef broth, 83–84
    canned, 151n, 153n
  black bean, 89–90
  chicken broth
    canned, 151n, 153n
    golden, 81–82
  goulash, 94–95
    with dumplings, 95
    thickened, 95
    unthickened, 94–95
  green split pea, 91–92
  ham bone for, 170n
  leek and potato, 85–87
  lentil, 88
  mushroom barley, 93
Sour cream
  chocolate layer cake, 220–222
  sauce, pheasant with, 146–148
Spinach soufflé, 187–188
Split pea soup, 91–92

Stew
Flemish beef, 152–153
venison, 153n
Storage, *see* at end of recipe
Strawberry shortcake, 216n
Striped bass
Eleanor, 122–123
stuffed, 119–121

T

Tart, caramel custard, 240–242
Tart shells
fillet of sole in, 73–75
prebaked, 27–29
Tarte tatin, 231
Temperature, conversion factor,
243–244
Toast ramekins, 52–61
anchovy pizza, 59
basic recipe, 52
cheese pizza, 59
crabmeat au gratin, 56–57
curried shrimp, 54–55
green pepper and onion pizza,
59
mushroom pizza, 60–61
sausage pizza, 59
tomato sauce for, 58
Tomato(es)
baked halves, 177–178
sauce, for pizza ramekins, 58
Tongue, braised, 158–159
Torte, frozen chocolate-coffee,
223–225
Travel & Leisure, 3

Turnovers
apricot, 237–238
cocktail, 64–70
basic recipe, 64–66
blue cheese, 70
Coney Island, 68–69
mushroom-onion, 67
pastry for, 64–65

U

Upside-down apple pie, 231–233
Utensils, 7–11
list of, 9–11
restaurant supply houses, 8

V

Veal
chops, braised, 160–161
country pâté, 71–72
stuffed breast of, 162–163
in stuffed cabbage, 171–173
Vegetable shortening for pastry,
22–23
Vegetables, 175–195
See also names of vegetables
Venison stew, 153n

W

Wafers, herbed cocktail, 50–51
White bread, 99–102

White-wine sauce, chicken in, 134–135
Whole wheat bread, 103–105
Williams, Richard L., 2
Wines, 14

Z

Zucchini, baked, 179